CALIBER RM 008-V2
TOURBILLON CHRONOGRAPH

Movement plate in carbon fibre
Hand-wound titanium movement
Split-second mecanism
with improved function
Power reserve
Torque indicator
Balance wheel with variable inertia
Fast rotating barrel
Barrel pawl with progressive recoil
Hair spring with special curve
New generation of escapement
Modular hand setting mechanism
Function indicator
Tooth system of barrel and third-wheel
pinion with central involute profile
Water resistant to 50 meters

GRAND COMPLICATIONS

THE ORIGINAL ANNUAL OF THE WORLD'S WATCH COMPLICATIONS AND MANUFACTURERS ®

First published in the United States in 2005 by:
TOURBILLON INTERNATIONAL LLC
11 West 25th Street, 8th floor
New York, NY 10010
T: +1 (212) 627-7732 Fax: +1 (212) 627-9093
www.tourbillon-watches.com

CHAIRMAN Joseph Zerbib

CHIEF EXECUTIVE OFFICER & PUBLISHER Caroline Childers

EDITOR Roberta Naas

MANAGING EDITOR Elizabeth Kindt

ART DIRECTOR Franca Vitali

DIRECTOR OF FINANCE Elliott Elbaz

In association with RIZZOLI INTERNATIONAL PUBLICATIONS INC.

300 Park Avenue South, New York, NY 10010

ISBN: 0-8478-2755-0

DISCLAIMER: THE INFORMATION CONTAINED IN *GRAND COMPLICATIONS* HAS BEEN PROVIDED BY THIRD PARTIES. WHILE WE BELIEVE THESE SOURCES TO BE RELIABLE, WE ASSUME NO RESPONSIBILITY OR LIABILITY FOR THE ACCURACY OF TECHNICAL DETAILS CONTAINED IN THIS BOOK.

EVERY EFFORT HAS BEEN MADE TO LOCATE THE COPYRIGHT HOLDERS OF MATERIALS PRINTED IN THIS BOOK. SHOULD THERE BE ANY ERRORS OR OMISSIONS, WE APOLOGIZE AND SHALL BE PLEASED TO MAKE ACKNOWLEDGEMENTS IN FUTURE EDITIONS.

PRINTED IN ITALY

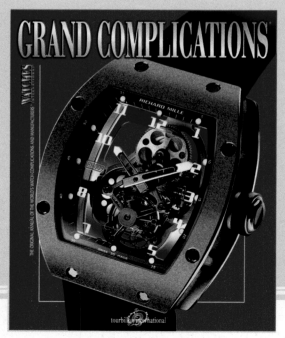

Grand Complications

VINTAGE 1945

TOURBILLON SOUS TROIS PONTS D'OR, AUTOMATIQUE

GP
GIRARD-PERREGAUX

ZENITH

SWISS WATCH MANUFACTURE

SINCE 1865

* From woman comes light.

STAR
Tourbillon
El Primero

"De la femme
vient la lumière*

LOUIS ARAGON

LETTER FROM THE PUBLISHER

To Collector '005:

The average watch collection is substantial enough for the owner to change his or her timepiece each day or night, depending on his humor, outfit, or needs based on weather or activity. Gold, steel and platinum cases are adorned with diamonds, rubies, and sapphires, various displays, in rounded or angular shapes—the aesthetic combinations are positively endless.

But of course, it takes more than a pretty case to seduce the savvy Collector '005—it's what's inside that sparks a love affair between a man and his watch: the caliber, function and precision of the movement. Grand complications by Audemars Piguet, a Breguet tourbillon, Girard-Perregaux's three gold Bridges, Richard Mille RM 009, a Vacheron Constantin or Zenith masterpiece—these are the watches that speak to the appreciative connoisseur.

A person must leave his chateau in France, his boat in the marina and his Ferrari in the garage, but he will wear his watch everywhere.

And so it is for you, Collector '005, that we at Tourbillon International have amassed this collection of "the best of the best" complicated timepieces from the world's leaders of haute horology. We hope you enjoy this first volume of Watches International: Grand Complications.

Caroline Childers

HARRY WINSTON

• RARE TIMEPIECES •

THE ART OF WATCHMA

*The revolving moon
perpetual calender
double barrel*

DE BETHUNE AMERICA (305) 695 1435

KING AT 21st CENTURY

The monopusher cronograph

GRAND COMPLICATIONS

THE ORIGINAL ANNUAL OF THE WORLD'S WATCH COMPLICATIONS AND MANUFACTURERS ®

TOURBILLON INTERNATIONAL, LLC

ADMINISTRATION, ADVERTISING SALES,
EDITORIAL, BOOK SALES

11 West 25th Street, 8th Floor
New York, NY 10010
T: +1 (212) 627-7732 Fax: +1 (212) 627-9093
www.tourbillon-watches.com
sales@tourbillon-watches.com

CHAIRMAN
Joseph Zerbib

CHIEF EXECUTIVE OFFICER & PUBLISHER
Caroline Childers
cchilders@tourbillon-watches.com

EDITOR
Roberta Naas

MANAGING EDITOR
Elizabeth Kindt
Elizabeth@tourbillon-watches.com

CONTRIBUTING EDITORS
Deborah Cohen, Roland Murphy,
Caroline Ruitz

ART DIRECTOR
Franca Vitali

DIRECTOR PRESS
Maurizio Zinelli

BUSINESS INTELLIGENCE & WEB MASTER
Marcel Choukroun

TRANSLATIONS
Igino Schraffl

DIRECTOR OF FINANCE
Elliott Elbaz

INTERNATIONAL ADVISOR
John Simonian

WEB DISTRIBUTION
www.amazon.com

PHOTOGRAPHIC ARCHIVES
Property of Tourbillon International, LLC

LETTER FROM THE EDITOR

Welcome to the first edition of *Grand Complications*. This very special book chronicles the most incredible feats in watchmaking. Centuries ago talented craftsmen and inventors toiled long days, weeks, months and even years to perfect the tracking of time.

In the 1500s horologists wrestled with replacing weights within clocks with springs to make clocks smaller and more accurate. Two centuries later, master watchmakers were dealing with perfecting escapements, making timepieces slimmer and more sturdy, and adding functions such as chimes, used to indicate the time after dark. In the late 1700s, some of the greatest watchmakers emerged Paul Leschot, Pierre Jaquet Droz, Abraham-Louis Breguet each of whom was intent on perfecting timekeeping and spent years developing new inventions. During this time, watchmaking feats included the tourbillon, the perpetual calendar (allowing for leap year), the gong spring and others. Since then, so many wonderful evolutions have occurred based on these foundations.

This book is designed to showcase present-day marvels. There are always new ways to do things, new displays to be designed, more precise timing to be achieved. These are the challenges that face today's finest watchmakers who still toil long days, weeks, months and even years to perfect a particular aspect of a particular watch. Despite the advancements of high-technology, mechanical watches reign supreme as stunning masterpieces works of art whose hearts easily comprise hundreds and hundreds of tiny pieces.

The pages herein present the most complex and complicated works of art for the wrist. Segmented by complication, with a complete description of the origins and new developments of each category, this book defines complicated watchmaking and offers a close-up look at technical marvels. So complex are some of these watches that many are made in limited editions or as one-of-kinds.

While there are many other complicated watches on the market, the editorial team of *Grand Complications* elected to present only those watchmakers and brands that are complete Manufactures, that is, brands who create their own movements in-house and present them in superb finished form. We invite you into the book and into the heart of complicated watches.

Roberta Naas

PARMIGIANI
SWISS MASTERPIECES

Tourbillon 30 seconds

PARMIGIANI
FLEURIER

WESTIME
BEVERLY HILLS, CA

What distinguishes Westime is our variety of selection and our customer service," says Savina Shivaee, a manager at Westime Watches in Los Angeles. "Customer service is our number-one goal."

The preeminent watch retailer in Southern California, Westime, which for the past 16 years has been providing some of the world's most illustrious watch aficionados with the most elite timepieces in creation, recently unveiled its new boutique on famed Rodeo Drive in Beverly Hills. As the exclusive U.S. distributor of the Richard Mille line of mechanical watches, Westime and its staff offer the watch lover an extraordinary experience: unsurpassed quality in a fabled, relaxed and comfortable environment.

Westime's watches range in price from $200 to $500,000, and while Shivaee says that Westime attracts "all kinds of people and truly has something for everyone," she explains that most of Westime's clientele are repeat customers, many of whom are watch collectors. Because of its selection and service, Westime has always attracted Hollywood's most famous faces, sports celebrities and world-class travelers. The Rodeo Drive salon—which echoes the sophisticated timepiece-themed décor of the original store on West Pico Boulevard—is smaller in scale, but still places a huge emphasis on service.

Very few places in the world sell watches that cost as much as a car, or sometimes a home. Westime does. Westime offers to clients some of the most rare and precious watches ever created who often travel halfway around the globe to shop there. Westime's service is so specialized that shopping can even be deemed therapeutic.

BRANDS CARRIED
AUDEMARS PIGUET
BREGUET
BREITLING
DE GRISOGONO
FRANCK MULLER
GLASHÜTTE
HARRY WINSTON
IWC
JAQUET DROZ
PARMIGIANI FLEURIER
RICHARD MILLE
URWERK
VERTU

Westime's staff combines to represent many cultures, enabling Westime to better serve its international clientele. Shivaee speaks three languages (English, Farsi and Spanish); staff members are fluent in a total of 10 languages. It is not unusual for a Westime staff member to meet clients at the airport or to drop off clients' watches at their homes. "There is no such thing as too much service," says Westime's owner, a second-generation watchmaker and one of the industry's foremost experts. "We are here to serve."

"For our customers, Westime is like a candy store," Shivaee says. "Some customers get overwhelmed by our selection." Westime is the authorized dealer of such brands as Audemars Piguet, Blancpain, Chopard, Franck Muller, Girard-Perregaux, Glashütte, Harry Winston and Vacheron Constantin, to name a few. "We carry an array of watch brands to accommodate all of our clients. Often men who purchase watches for themselves will want to purchase jewelry for their wives," Shivaee explains. The latest trend is towards bigger watches, Shivaee observes, and also mechanical watches. "I find people are actually looking for evening watches, even though no one cares what time it is when they are out for the evening," she adds. Like her customers, Shivaee simply adores watches. "Every time a new line comes out, I fall in love with it," she says. While Shivaee likes to wear whatever is new ("I change with the wind," she says), her husband prefers vintage watches. Westime caters to this wide range of tastes, offering limited editions and special order pieces. And although a truly fabulous watch will usually have a price tag to match, Westime clients would say it's well worth it. After all, as Shivaee points out, "What is the face you look at most?"

254 North Rodeo Drive, Beverly Hills, CA 90210
Tel: 310.271.0000   Fax: 310.271.3091
www.westimewatches.com

1889. When The Eiffel Tower in Paris was built, Vacheron Constantin was 134 years old.

...DEDICATED TO PERFECTION

LL-Roger-Viollet

OPENWORKED TOURBILLON
Hand-wound mechanical movement with Tourbillon Regulator, openworked and chased by hand. Power reserve of more than 45 hours and analog date calendar. Case in 18K pink gold with transparent back. Glareproofed crystal. Hands in black oxidized 18K gold.

30067/000R-8954

www.vacheron-constantin.com

VACHERON CONSTANTIN

Manufacture Horlogère. Genève, depuis 1755.

DARAKJIAN JEWELERS
SOUTHFIELD, MI

Few jewelers can boast what this Southfield, Michigan retailer has to offer. Darakjian Jewelers recently celebrated 40 years of service-driven business with its founding father still actively at the helm.

John Darakjian first opened his jewelry store door in October 1964 in the once-famed Metropolitan Building in downtown Detroit. Early on, Darakjian built an incredibly loyal following of customers from all walks of life. That clientele has remained steadfast in its commitment to this family-owned firm, and the owners of Darakjian remain faithful to them. At 74 years old, John still enjoys laughing and talking with the customers who first made his business a success four decades ago.

Indeed, John Darakjian, along with his wife Bergy and sons Ara and Armen, are dedicated to offering a three-prong approach to keeping customers and friends happy: service, selection and a comfortable, uplifting atmosphere. Service before, during, and after sales is key. While some stores use the words service-oriented as a marketing buzz-word, Darakjian lives by it. Service is the thread that holds the store together. Darakjian guarantees 24-hour repairs and 72-hour appraisals, or they're free. The sales staff is incredibly knowledgeable, with on-going training and a passion about their products.

BRANDS CARRIED	
AUDEMARS PIGUET	MONTBLANC
BELL & ROSS	MOVADO
BLANCPAIN	PHILIP STEIN
CHOPARD	RADO
GLYCINE	TECHNOMARINE
GUCCI	TISSOT
HUBLOT	ULYSSE NARDIN
LONGINES	VACHERON CONSTANTIN

Selection is equally as important. According to Armen Darakjian, "We offer something different, unique, in all price ranges, things the savvy customer can't find anywhere else."

Indeed, in addition to its custom jewelry and elegant lines, Darakjian Jewelers carries approximately 16 watch brands in its store. The brands range in price so that the jeweler is sure to have something for every one of its customers, no matter their profession or spending range. Among the best-selling brands at the store: Audemars Piguet, Blancpain, Chopard, Gucci, Movado, Rado, Ulysse Nardin, Vacheron Constantin. These tried-and-trues are complemented by some high-tech brands including Bell & Ross, Philip Stein and TechnoMarine.

The store's customer-friendly service and selection policy is backed by a champagne and cappuccino bar and its "concierge-on-Saturdays" approach. At any given time, juices, champagne and cappuccino are served to customers in a relaxed setting. On Saturdays, a concierge works the store, happy to help with plans for dinner, events and the like. The store's atmosphere is a superb blend of contemporary and traditional thanks to the colorful, geometric balance and warm wood cases. It is at once comfortable and relaxing. At one end of the store is an elegant boutique area dedicated to three of the more luxurious brands: Audemars Piguet, Ulysse Nardin and Vacheron Constantin.

Even Darakjian's approach to thanking its clients and to marketing and advertising is unique. VIPS were treated to a huge, fabulous party held in honor of the brand's 40 years and special anniversary promotions were offered to members of the community.

Indeed, everything this jeweler embraces—from customers to products, marketing and events—is done with a fervent emphasis on personalized service, to preserving friendships and relationships that can last for decades to come. It is this honest, down-to-earth approach that has earned Darakjian Jeweler its distinguished reputation.

29333 Northwestern Highway, Southfield, MI 48034
Tel: 888.843.6659
www.darakjian.com

The completion of a Langematik Perpetual requires several months of precision craftsmanship.

The making of the movement of the Langematik Perpetual.
The master watchmakers at Lange assemble each movement twice – part by part, with the utmost concentration. The enormous amount of additional work involved in the disassembly and reassembly processes is necessary to guarantee the absolutely flawless functionality of this highly complicated timekeeping mechanism. The same meticulous care is applied to the micron-accurate production of the 478 individual parts and the time-consuming artistic decoration of their surfaces, even on those sides that later remain concealed to the eye of the beholder.

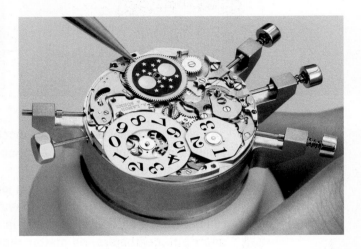

A. LANGE
GLASHÜT

In 1845, Adolph Lange gave up his privileged position as the watchmaker to the royal Saxon court and ventured into the impoverished mining town of Glashütte in the Ore Mountains to establish the German precision watchmaking industry. He developed totally new preci- sion tools, invented innovative mechanisms and manu- facturing methods, and began to craft watches for per- petuity. In the course of time, he created unique master- pieces of inestimable value, many of which today can be admired in prestigious public and private collections. Subsequently, for 100 years, the watches of "A. Lange & Söhne" were among the most sought-after in the world, until the division of Germany eradicated the proud company's name on timepiece dials. "A. Lange & Söhne" became a legend. But immediately after German reuni-

Then it's ready for eternity.

The Langematik-Perpetual.
A masterpiece made for eternity. The calendar of the Langematik Perpetual will display the correct date, day of week, and month until 1 March 2100 at which time the date will have to be manually advanced by one day. And 122 years will elapse before its moon-phase display deviates from the true synodic month by one day. The Langematik Perpetual is graced with a delicately embossed three-quarter winding rotor made of platinum and gold. It features Lange's patented zero-reset mechanism and comes in a precious 18-carat gold or platinum case that will endure the passage of time.

& SÖHNE
TE I/SA

fication, Walter Lange, Adolph Lange's great-grandson, returned to Glashütte to once again demonstrate the prowess of Lange watchmaking artistry with the same love of innovation that originally made Lange famous around the globe. And as in the old days, Lange's unique watches are still painstakingly crafted and assembled by hand. Lange watches will always be exclusive, as are the few jewellers in the world that offer "A. Lange & Söhne" masterpieces. There, connoisseurs of watchmaking excellence can find a catalogue documenting the inge- nious creations of "A. Lange & Söhne" and the company's legacy – as is only fitting when a legend comes back to life. General Agent for A. Lange & Söhne: Richemont North America Inc., 645 Fifth Avenue, 10022 New York, NY, phone (212) 891 2355. www.lange-soehne.com.

Summary

AP
AUDEMARS PIGUET
Le maître de l'horlogerie depuis 1875

JD

JAQUET DROZ

ART HORLOGER DEPUIS 1738

LES DOUZE VILLES
HOMMAGE LA CHAUX-DE-FONDS 1738

Web Site Directory

A. Lange & Söhne	www.alange-soehne.com	Guy Ellia:	www.guyellia.com
Arnold & Son:	www.arnoldandson.com	Harry Winston:	www.harry-winston.com
Audemars Piguet:	www.audemarspiguet.com	IWC:	www.iwc.ch
Baume & Mercier:	www.baume-et-mercier.com	Jaeger-LeCoultre:	www.jaeger-lecoultre.com
Blancpain:	www.blancpain.com	Jaquet Droz:	www.jaquet-droz.com
Bovet:	www.bovet-fleurier.ch	Kiu Tai Yu:	www.kiutaiyu.com
Breguet:	www.breguet.com	Parmigiani Fleurier:	www.parmigiani.com
Breitling:	www.breitling.com	Patek Philippe:	www.patek-philippe.ch
Bvlgari:	www.bulgari.com	Piaget:	www.piaget.com
Cartier:	www.cartier.com	RGM:	www.rgmwatches.com
Chopard:	www.chopard.com	Roger Dubuis:	www.roger-dubuis.com
Corum:	www.corum.ch	Ulysse Nardin:	www.ulysse-nardin.com
De Bethune:	www.debethune.ch	Vacheron Constantin:	
de Grisogono:	www.degrisogono.com		www.vacheron-constantin.com
Eberhard & Co.:	www.eberhard-co-watches.ch	Zenith:	www.zenith-watches.ch
F.P. Journe:	www.fpjourne.com		
Franck Muller:	www.franckmullerusa.com	**RELATED SITES**	
Gérald Genta:	www.geraldgenta.com	Tourbillon International:	
Girard-Perregaux:	www.girard-perregaux.ch		www.tourbillon-watches.com
Glashütte Original:	www.glashuette.de	BaselWorld:	www.baselworld.com
Graham:	www.graham-london.com	Auctions:	www.christies.com
Greubel Forsey:	www.greubelforsey.ch		www.sothebys.com

INDEX

MOD. 1 RTM *DIAMONDS*

TO WIND UP ONE
AUTOMATIC WRISTWATCH

SCATOLA
del
TEMPO ®

the first, the only, the original one.

S.C.S. & Co. Via dei Mille 17 - 23891 Barzanò (LC) - Tel. 039 95 52 60 - Fax 039 95 89 70

W
Ä

RICHARD MILLE

A RACING MACHINE ON THE WRIST

CALIBER RM 003-V2

DUAL TIME TOURBILLON

Movement plate in carbon fibre
Hand-wound movement
Power reserve
Torque indicator
Variable inertia balance
Fast rotating barrel
Second time zone
Function selector
Available in platinum, white gold,
pink gold and titanium

THE MAGIC
OF MECHANICS

By Roberta Naas

From furs to fine wines, from diamonds to rubies – luxury is all about touch, taste, feel or looks. But for the very savvy connoisseur, luxury and exclusivity are perhaps most coveted in the form of fine mechanics. No luxury automobile collector could resist the sound of the engine of a Saleen S7, a Rolls Royce or Bentley. But many have to wait to own these exclusive beauties.

Similarly, the world's finest watches purr with precision – and capture the hearts of collectors around the world. How many a fine timepiece has sold at auction for upwards of a million dollars? The numbers are higher than could be counted on one's hands and feet. Even new timepieces – created in today's world – that command prices in the quarter-million-dollar range have a waiting list of buyers.

Indeed, in a world of quartz and solar watches, of electronic gadgetry and computer miniaturization and saturation –– mechanical timepieces weave a web of magic for those in the know.

It was centuries ago that the tourbillon was developed by Breguet to balance the effects of gravity on a pocket watch; it was even earlier that the repeater watch chimed the time in the dark for European or Asian aristocrats. Still, with the advent of new technology, these mechanical feats remain coveted in today's watches – perhaps because it takes one master watch-maker hundreds, sometimes thousands of hours, to build and assemble all the tiny parts into a small disk that fits on the wrist.

What's more — and this is the magical part — those tiny pieces keep on working and working and working – despite black outs and computer viruses. One might wonder what drives a watchmaker to keep creating watches with several hundred tiny parts in them. What is the impetus behind a watch with practically the entire northern hemisphere's constellation on it – in superb working order, one might add. These questions seem simple when posed the finest master watchmakers in Switzerland. Answers range from, "because we can" to "because it is a legacy that has been passed down from our forefathers" and to "because there are collectors who have an insatiable desire for these masterpieces."

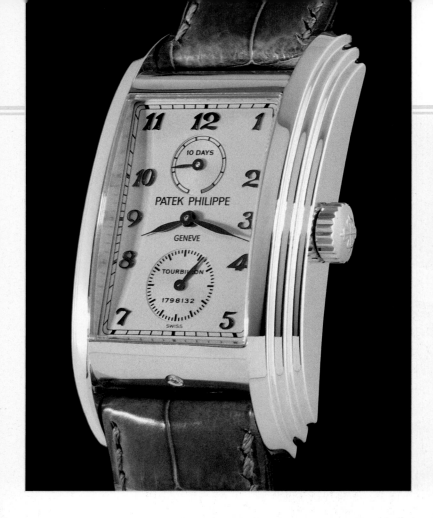

All of these answers further underscore the very essence of this book. Master watchmakers from the worlds' finest watch manufactures — those who create their own parts, movements and finished complicated timepieces — toil tirelessly to present superb specimens of timekeeping today that are destined to be the next centuries' coveted watches at auction. So, what are these masterpieces? Complexities of all mechanical types: tourbillons, repeaters, sonneries, perpetual calendars, equations of time and grand complications that incorporate several of these watchmaking accomplishments.

These complexities demand unsurpassed standards of excellence in craftsmanship and only a treasured couple of handfuls of watch brands rise to those challenges. The Manufactures that create their own movements in their workshops, that build part upon part within a watch — are the brands featured in this book.

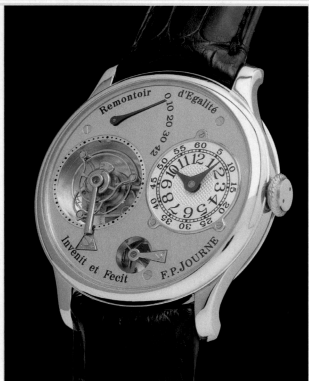

The watches herein can take weeks, months or even years to produce and most are created in very limited numbers, if not as one-of-a-kinds. In some instances, a Manufacture may only produce, for instance, seven of a certain model – and those seven watches must be spread to retailers around the world. The selection process of which retailer receives one of these beauties is a difficult one, but it is based on which retailer has the clientele to purchase such a superb item. What's more, it's not unusual to find a waiting list for one of these masterpieces – a waiting list that is based on either a "first come, first served," motto, or simply on time – the time it takes to create more of the particular watch. Often, only a few lucky collectors will ever own one of the most complicated timepieces built. Others complications are created in more accessible numbers, such as perpetual calendars, split-second chronographs or multiple time zone pieces.

The watches in this book are the watches that museums are made of, that auctions are made of and that the future of watchmaking are made of. The pages in this book feature manufactures of these magical wonders and their newest acts. Indulge.

250 YEARS STRONG

By Roberta Naas

The grand house of Vacheron Constantin celebrates its 250th anniversary in 2005. It is a quarter-millennium anniversary rich with heritage for the oldest continually operated Swiss watch brand. In honor of this distinctive occasion, the brand celebrates in a manner worthy of its past and indicative of its future: It has created an incredible 250th anniversary watch collection teeming with complications.

Each of Vacheron Constantin's five key models has a production run representing the year of the manufacture's birth—1,755 pieces—and each is a true collector's item. Created as a single piece is a spectacular 100mm 18-karat gold-and-sapphire case. It features a clock at the center of a global sphere behind eight gold petals that open to reveal the clock. Only the owner of this watch will know how to operate the mechanism that opens the sphere.

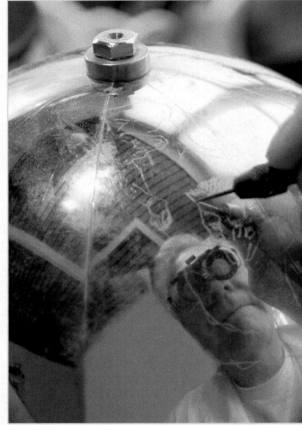

A work of multi-disciplines, this L'Esprit des Cabinotiers clock was two years in the research and development stages. The one-of-a-kind piece is created in the sprit of the watchmaking cabinotiers of Vacheron Constantin's early days. The mystery clock, which rests on a base of sapphire, onyx and lapis lazuli, offers a second time zone, perpetual calendar, quarter repeater on request, power reserve, moonphase, equation of time, astronomical indicator and thermometer.

The incredibly beautiful astronomical signs have been hand enameled in the old-world technique on the outer rim of the dial. Similarly, the outer 18-karat rose-gold sphere has been hand engraved with the zodiac signs in an antique pattern fashioned after a design reminiscent of 1755. All of the engraving was done by one master engraver and took approximately four months to complete. The key-wound mechanism that opens the lotus-like petals of the sphere is hidden in the base of the clock and consists of 580 pieces.

The dial of the watch is also 18-karat gold and was entirely hand guillochéd. It features nearly 800 individually etched lines. The moonphase indicator, crafted of gold and lapis lazuli, took a week of hand engraving to achieve the realistic face. Indeed in this one timepiece, Vacheron Constantin has commingled the true art of craftsmanship in superior harmony with haute horology.

Other Vacheron Constantin masterpieces include the Tour de L'ile wristwatch—deemed by the brand to be the most complex wristwatch and featured in our Multi-Complications chapter. This watch is created in an edition of seven pieces. Comprising the 55 pieces is the Saint-Gervais tourbillon perpetual calendar watch, featured in our Tourbillon chapter. There is also a special 1755 Jubilee watch that the brand is creating in an edition of 1,755 pieces.

In addition to these timepieces, Vacheron Constantin has unveiled a special collection that heralds the brand's rich enamel-art history. The Métiers d' Art is sold as a set of four rich-

ly decorated watches in a box. Only 12 sets will be created. Each set houses the same 18-karat gold-and-enamel design on all four watches. Each watch, however, is created in a different metal—platinum, 18-karat white, yellow or rose gold—and each is enameled in colors representative of the four seasons.

According to Claude Proellochs, head of Vacheron Constantin worldwide, "These 250th-anniversary pieces are in addition to our newest collection, and represent the brands progressive know-how and ability to permanently challenge the limits and bring together watchmaking design with research and development for uniquely exceptional accomplishments."

Indeed, the complicated timepieces unveiled for the jubilee succinctly express the brand's motto: Do better if it is possible, and it is always possible.

de GRISOGONO®
GENEVE

INTRODUCING

INSTRUMENTO
GRANDE

GENEVA - PARIS - LONDON - GSTAAD - ROME - HONG KONG
KUWAIT - MOSCOW - NEW YORK - PORTO CERVO - ST MORITZ

de GRISOGONO®
GENEVE

PINK GOLD AUTOMATIC WATCH WITH DUAL TIME ZONE AND OVERSIZED DATE
BLACKENED MOVEMENT AND CROWN SET WITH A NATURAL BLACK DIAMOND

www.degrisogono.com

KIU TAI YU

By Elizabeth Kindt

A member of the Académie Horlogère
des Créateurs Indépendants, this multi-faceted
man has been linked with some of the most famous
master watchmakers in the world. A collector of
important pocket watches, a timepiece restorer,
retailer and even publisher, Kiu Tai Yu represents
the Far East take on watchmaking through
his entirely handmade single-piece tourbillons
from his strategic location in Hong Kong.

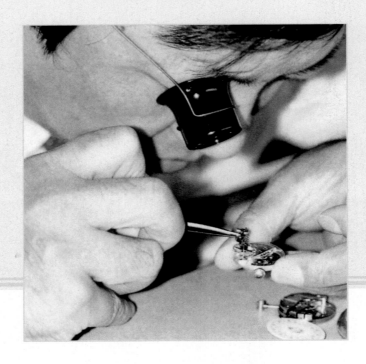

The watch dial reads: KIU'S MYSTERY TOURBILLON, N°10, with Chinese characters 香港 and 天儀軒.

Each watch by Kiu Tai Yu represents a trip into the Far East aesthetic. His most impressive creations include the Tourbillon Flying (the only example of a tourbillon semi-volant mechanism made for wristwatches) and the Mystery Tourbillon Rectangular. It is crafted in pink-, yellow- and white-gold volutes and a rectangular curved case that follows the curve of the wrist, recalling the ancient shapes of the pagoda. The Mystery Flying Tourbillon No. 12 (with tourbillon at 9:00, hour and minute off-center at 2:00) is also designed with classic decorative elements from the Chinese tradition, cleverly substituting the conventional minute markers of the dial and zones.

Tourbillon No. 13 includes the classic technical themes of this master watchmaker from the Orient: visible flying-tourbillon carriage and off-center hour indicator. In this particular example, the balance and balance-spring are off-center with respect to the tourbillon carriage and a six-mark-

er wheel is mounted on the escapement wheel. The tourbillon seems to hold no mysteries for Kiu Tai Yu, since he has explored virtually all of the possible technical solutions this complication allows, including the one with balance and balance-spring housed within the turning carriage and the escapement fastened to the fixed part of the movement. Furthermore, each individual—and therefore unique—watch is completely handmade and -produced.

Kiu Tai Yu's spectacular platinum Joy of the Millennium was inspired by the delicate mechanics of the Heavenly Clocks (i.e. the Chinese astronomical timepieces used more than 1,000 years ago) and is characterized by the large 18-karat gold sight balance-bridge and off-center hour display on a hand-decorated subdial. Its markers alternate between Roman, Arabic and Chinese numerals.

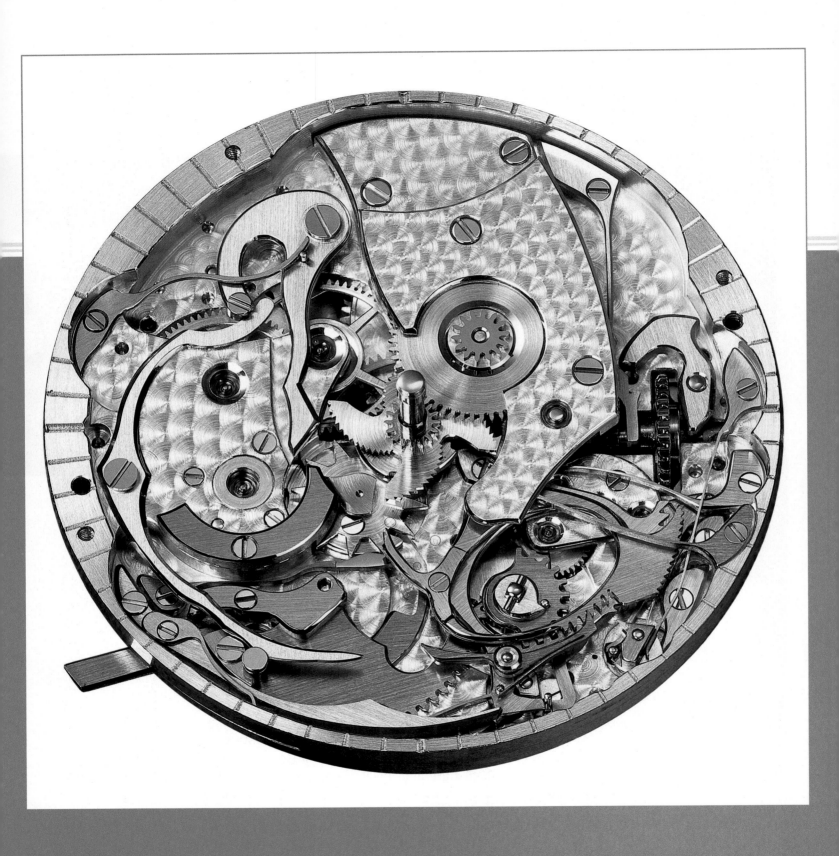

MULTI-COMPLICATIONS

A multi-complication is a timekeeping masterpiece. Likened to the finest paintings in the art world, multi-complication timepieces are created by the best master watchmakers in the world who pour thousands of hours into their creations. These incredible treasure often house hundreds and hundreds of miniscule parts in a case that fits beautifully on the wrist. What's more, those parts have been so perfectly planned, so exquisitely designed that they fit together seamlessly, maximized to their highest performance potential.

The Star Caliber offers 21 different watchmaking complications and six patented inventions

A multi-complication houses several of the most important watchmaking feats: tourbillon, repeater or sonnerie, equation of time, perpetual calendar, or chronograph rattrapante. In rare instances, they incorporate all of these functions and more. True works of art, multi-complications are often some of the most beautifully embellished timepieces on the outside as well, featuring dozens of carats of diamonds and gemstones. The number of man-hours that a single piece can require from start to finish is incredible.

Because of the workmanship involved, there is often a long waiting list for the most coveted multi-complications and only the most avid, aggressive collector will ever own one; they are made in such extremely limited numbers that demand clearly outweighs supply. Multi-complications have fetched millions of dollars at auctions.

Among the most notable multi-complications in history are Patek Philippe's Caliber 89, Patek Philippe's Graves Watch and IWC's II Destriero Scafusia—respected among the most complex timepieces in the world. Most recently, Vacheron Constantin unveiled its most complicated watch—possibly the most complicated wristwatch in the world—the Tour de L'Ile.

Only seven Tour de L'Ile watches will ever be created and each will house 834 individual parts and offer 16 complications that can be read off of a double-faced watch. The 47mm case houses the new Caliber 2750 with toubillon, minute repeater, moonphase, age of moon, perpetual calendar, second time zone, equation of time, sunrise, sunset, and sky chart. The watch was created in honor of the brand's 250th anniversary, celebrated in 2005.

In 1989, in honor of its 150th birthday, Patek Philippe produced the most complicated pocket watch in the world—the Caliber 89. This timepieces houses the tourbillon along with a myriad of other complicated functions and displays.

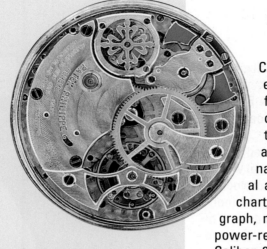

Caliber 89 bears 1,728 individual parts, two main dials, eight discs and 24 hands. Among the 33 timekeeping functions it performs are the hours, minutes and seconds in sidereal time (based on the earth's rotation), the times of sunrise and sunset, the equation of time, time in a different zone and split-second timing. This extraordinary watch also features tourbillon escapement, perpetual and secular calendar, astronomical calendar, celestial chart, the date of Easter, moonphase, split-seconds chronograph, minute repeater, grand strike and petite strike, alarm, power-reserve indicator and four-way setting system. The Caliber 89 required four years to develop, five years to hand assemble, features several other horological functions and offers one non-horological feature: a thermometer.

Another multi-complication from Patek Philippe is The Star Caliber, whose movement underwent eight-plus years in the invention and development stages. It houses thousands of tiny parts in a case less than three inches in diameter, and in its finished form costs more than $7 million. It follows Caliber 89 and the Graves Watch—a 24-complication pocket watch created for Henry Graves in 1933. The Star Caliber offers 21 watchmaking complications and six patented inventions. It is the first time in the history of Patek Philippe that one timepiece encased so many patents, including the cherished Westminster chimes, a sound never before fully achieved in a watch. The Star Caliber chimes the quarter-hours and full hours on five separate gongs with remarkable resonance. The watch also chimes the minutes, if so desired by the wearer. Additionally, patents exist or are pending for: the running equation of time; sunrise and sunset times; movements of the sky and moon; selective sprung-cover release mechanism; and the rapid calendar corrector. Two of Patek Philippe's prized master watchmakers dedicated 10 years solely to this project. The mechanical heart of each Star Caliber timepiece is an intricate masterpiece consisting of 1,118 individual microscopic parts.

While many brands find it difficult to measure up to the horological distinction of Patek Philippe's Caliber 89, the challenge has become life's work for those in pursuit of perfection.

Noted watchmaking greats Girard-Perregaux, IWC, Audemars Piguet, Vacheron Constantin, Franck Muller, Parmigiani Fleurier, Jaeger-LeCoultre, Jaquet Droz, De Bethune and a handful of others create incredible multi-complications.

Another one of the world's most complicated wristwatches is the Il Destriero Scafusia by IWC (International Watch Company). This watch in itself is an impressive horological accomplishment in the world of complex movements and technical prowess. The Il Destriero Scafusia's movement consists of 750 parts and has a total of 21 functions and displays. Dubbed the "war horse" by IWC, the watch features a tourbillon, perpetual calendar, split second chronograph with flyback hand, perpetual moonphase and an extravagant minute repeater. One of IWC's supreme achievements, the Il Destriero Scafusia was the first to house what is refered to today as a type of flying tourbillon. The escapement of this watch is also relieved of the effects of magnetism, as the tourbillon cage is made of antimagnetic titanium. The ball bearing-mounted flying tourbillon consists of more than 80 single parts yet weighs less than 0.03 gram.

Girard-Perregaux has been winning awards and respect in watchmaking for more than century, including gold medals at the Paris Exhibitions in 1867 and 1889. Included in its most recent collection of watchmaking feats are watches such as those belonging to the Opera series that offer different functions, most notably Westminster chime repeaters and Tourbillon with three gold Bridges.

Audemars Piguet's 1997 Grande Complication brought together in its 416 parts the minute repeater, split-second chronograph and perpetual calendar with moonphase. The company then garnished the piece with 288 brilliant diamonds, 96

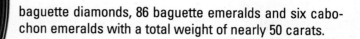

baguette diamonds, 86 baguette emeralds and six cabochon emeralds with a total weight of nearly 50 carats.

Blancpain's mastery of complication, the 1735, combines six master movements of the horological art into one watch: the ultra-slim mechanical movement, the perpetual calendar, moonphase, tourbillon, minute repeater and split-second chronograph.

Franck Muller created a very unique watch in 1992's World Premiere. Muller combined the minute repeater, grande and petite sonnerie, perpetual calendar to the year 2100, moonphase, and retrograde equation of time into the watch, which was crafted from a single block of 950 platinum. Muller further complicated the World Premiere in 1995 by adding a tourbillon to the watch.

Most recently, Jaeger-LeCoultre unveiled the stunning multi-complication called the Gyrotourbillon I. Retailing at approximately $300,000 (USD based on conversion rates) this spectacular achievement is crafted in platinum, and features a patented spherical tourbillon that beats much like a heart. It also houses one of the most difficult watchmaking complications—a running equation of time. Essentially, equation of time indicates the difference between the average sun day and the true sun day. (In reality, time is not consistent from one day to the next in relation to the meridian. In order to have consistency, all of the days in a year were calculated and an average sun day of 24 hours was determined. However, the true sun day can vary from just over 14 minutes to 16 minutes on certain days of the year. The equation of time displays the difference on a daily basis.)

The Gyrotourbillon I also offers perpetual date via two retrograde indicators and a retrograde perpetual indication of the month and leap year on the back of the watch. The development and creation of the Gyrotourbillon I took nearly four years. Nearly four days are required to simply assemble the tourbillon escapements, and four weeks to assemble the entire timepiece. Only 25 pieces will be made per year and no more than 75 pieces total.

AUDEMARS PIGUET - JULES AUDEMARS GRANDE COMPLICATION

REF. 258660R

The Jules Audemars Grande Complication houses the self-winding caliber 2885 with more than 600 components. The watch offers perpetual calendar, minute repeater, and split-second chronograph. It is housed in 18-karat pink gold and features five correctors and a slide for the repeater on the side. The month and four-year cycle are positioned at 6:00 and the moonphase and date are shown at 12:00. This watch is also available in platinum.

AUDEMARS PIGUET - ROYAL OAK GRAND COMPLICATION

The Royal Oak Grand Complication houses the self-winding caliber 2885, 13.5-line movement and features a split-seconds chronograph, a minute repeater and a perpetual calendar with day of the week indication. A subdial for the seconds is offered at 9:00. Cased in 18-karat gold, the movement beats at a steady 19,800 vibrations per hour. Twelve indicators are on the dial, including current year, leap-year indicator and moonphase readout. The movement is a labyrinth of 654 parts.

BREGUET - CLASSIQUE TOURBILLON PERPETUAL CALENDAR

Boasting a tourbillon, perpetual calendar, engine-turning, Breguet blued hands and a Serpentine hand, off-center main dial and subdials, and cannelé middle, this complicated watch represents—in pure old-fashioned Breguet style—the entire set of shapes used by the most prolific inventor and innovator of ancient pocket watches. The Breguet 558QPT caliber based on a Lemania 187 added with a module for the perpetual indication of day, date, month and leap year, reproduces the excitement that kings and queens have experienced through Breguet's masterpieces for years.

DE BETHUNE - CS2

This 18-karat rose-gold timepiece is a masterful work of horological tradition. It houses a tourbillon, minute repeater, equation of time, and perpetual calendar. The tourbillon is visible through the sapphire caseback. The repeater function is fitted with a strike-silent mechanism and the gongs are tuned with each hammer. The equation of time is measured by the rose-gold center hand and calculated with the latest astronomic indications. The 319-part manual-winding mechanism houses 20 jewels, a Swiss lever escapement, and Breguet spring balance. The mechanism is decorated with the Côtes de Genève pattern and offers 30 hours of power reserve. The dial is silver with hand-guillochéd pattern. The rose-gold date display is at 7:30 and month display is at 4:30.

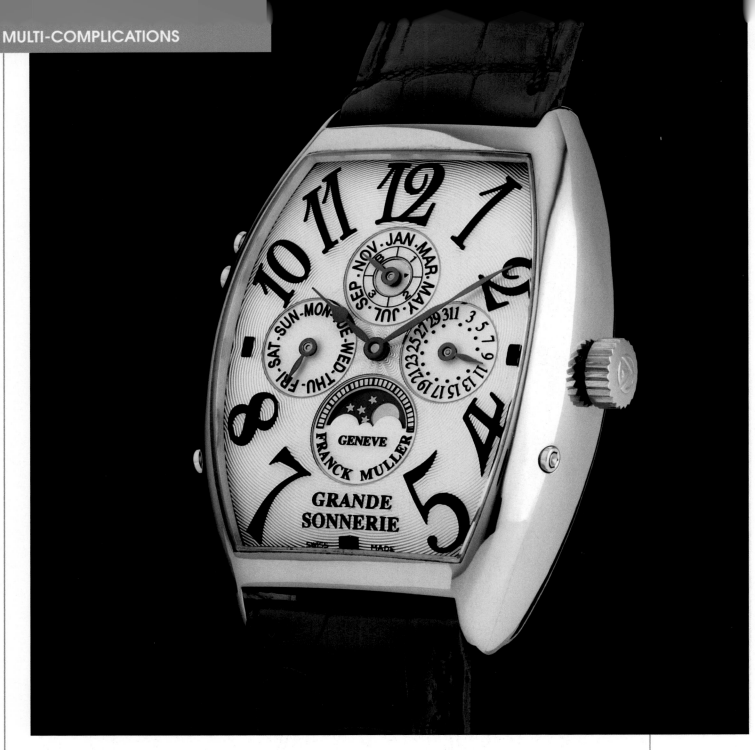

FRANCK MULLER - CINTRÉE CURVEX GRANDE AND PETITE SONNERIE PERPETUAL CALENDAR

The manual-winding Franck Muller caliber RFM 7850 offers repeater, grand and petite sonnerie, and perpetual calendar. Along with the classic minute repeater, it is provided with the rare sonnerie "au passage," function. The grande sonnerie indicates the hours through a sequence of low tones, and strikes the hours and quarters at the passage of the quarters (the latter with two tones, one high- and one low-pitched). The petite sonnerie strikes only the hours. On the case's left side is the slide for the actuation of the hour, quarter and minute repeater, and the cursor for the selection of the sonnerie modes (grande, petite and mute). The 500-part movement has 50 jewels and two barrels that allow bidirectional crown winding: counterclockwise for the movement, clockwise for the sonnerie.

Grand Complications

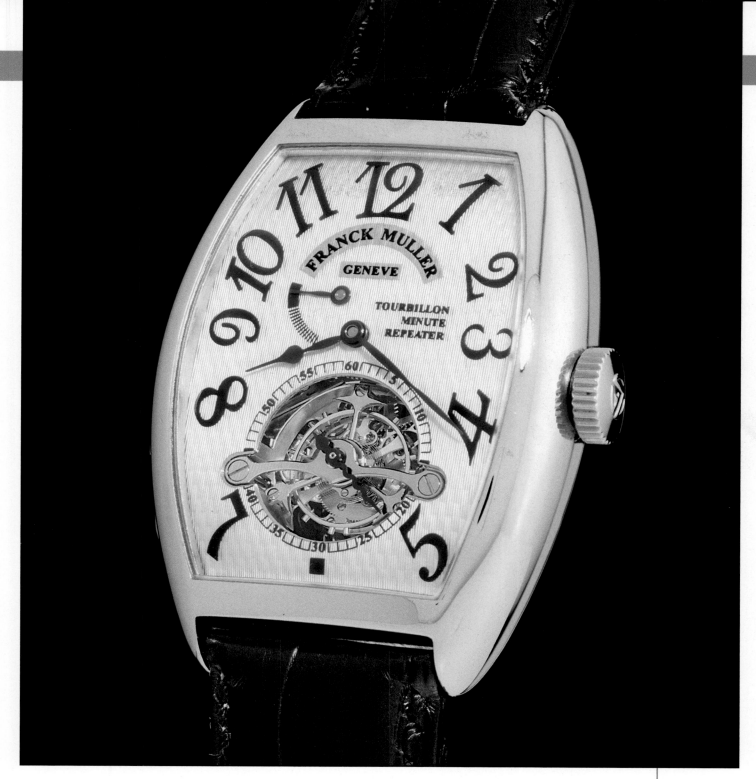

FRANCK MULLER - CINTRÉE CURVEX REPEATER TOURBILLON IMPERIALE

The manual-winding Franck Muller caliber. TRM95 features the tourbillon and minute repeater. This complicated watch from the Cintrée Curvex family is equipped with a shaped movement developed inside Franck Muller's workshop and features a patented device indicating the end of the strike-work ringing. It consists of a hand indicating that the relevant wheels have reached their idle positions, so as to avoid sending untimely requests to the repeater mechanism. The movement is displayed through a dial-side window.

FRANCK MULLER - CINTRÉE CURVEX TOURBILLON CHRONOGRAPH IMPERIALE

The manual-winding Franck Muller caliber TFC01 houses the tourbillon and chronograph with two counters. The movement of this watch of great esthetic and technical fascination is a chronograph caliber equipped with an "integrated tourbillon device" (meaning the movement is not made up by a base, called time base, and additional modules, but the different complications are integrated in the movement itself). In this case, the chronograph components are arranged in such a way as to avoid interfering with the tourbillon system positioned at 6:00. The tourbillon carriage shows the knife-edge pattern that appeared for the first time on the model without complications. The chronograph is provided with a column wheel, assuring a perfect synchronization of the following modes: start, stop and zeroing. The watch's autonomy is 72 hours.

GÉRALD GENTA - GRANDE SONNERIE 99

This manual-winding caliber GG 31000 offers tourbillon, grand and petite sonneries, minute repeater and double power reserve. The Grande Sonnerie model, presented for the first time in 1994, was reworked for this new version for the 30th anniversary of the Gérald Genta brand. The very limited space of this wristwatch's movement with off-center hour display, tourbillon and two barrels also houses the repeater mechanisms and the "au passage" strike-work with a four-hammer Westminster chime. On the caseback, there are subdials for the power reserve (movement and sonnerie) and for the sonnerie mode selection (grande, petite, mute).

GIRARD-PERREGAUX - OPERA ONE REF. 99760

Considered a true masterpiece, the Opera One was first released in the year 2000. It features a carillon Westminster, minute repeater, and Tourbillon with three gold Bridges. To increase the mystery and appeal of the Opera One, the watchmakers at Girard-Perregaux revealed the hammers of the striking mechanism and the tourbillon through small apertures on the dial. The magnificent watch houses the manual-winding GP9899 caliber with 75 hours of power reserve.

GIRARD-PERREGAUX - OPERA TWO REF. 99740

The Opera Two features a perpetual calendar in addition to the carillon Westminster, minute repeater, and Tourbillon with three gold Bridges. The Opera Two is housed in a case of pink, yellow, or white gold, or in platinum. Three of the four strike hammers are visible through the dial. The fourth hammer can be seen only when the striking mechanism is operated. The extraordinary complexity of the refined tourbillon movement can be admired through the watch's sapphire caseback. The perpetual calendar indicates the hours and minutes, the day of the week, dates and months, as well as the leap-year cycle. The GP9897 caliber offers 80 hours of power reserve, and beats at 21,600 vibrations per hour.

GIRARD-PERREGAUX - SPLIT-SECOND CHRONOGRAPH MINUTE REPEATER

This manual-winding Girard-Perregaux caliber 9898 offers tourbillon, minute repeater and split-second chronograph with two counters. This large (Ø 40mm) timepiece, produced by the workshops of La Chaux-de-Fonds, is provided with a particular repeater slide and a winding crown acting also as a pusher for the split-second chronograph. The chronograph mechanisms—especially the chronograph column wheel on the top, the split-second chronograph at the bottom and its U-shaped chuck enclosing the split-second wheel at the center—are displayed through the sapphire crystal in the foreground. On the lower level, the tourbillon device and the repeater hammers are displayed. The model is realized with only a cream-colored dial and in a very limited annual series.

GIRARD-PERREGAUX - TOURBILLON WITH THREE GOLD BRIDGES

This manual-winding Girard-Perregaux caliber 9892-070 features the tourbillon and minute repeater. Here, the three solid pink-gold Bridges of the tourbillon are displayed through the transparent caseback and are skeletonized and chased by hand with a great arabesque pattern. Gear wheels are provided with wolf-teeth, as they were in the Sous Trois Ponts d'Or pocket watch of 1867, which won the gold medal at the Paris World Exhibition that year and in 1889. The case is adorned with diamonds set on the flange, bezel, lugs and crown.

GIRARD-PERREGAUX - VINTAGE 1945 MAGISTRAL TOURBILLON REF. 99710

Housing the remontage manual-winding GP09700.3950 movement, this stunning Vintage 1945 Magistral Tourbillon boasts astonishing features that delight both the eye and the ear. The Tourbillon with gold Bridge is visible through the dial aperture at 6:00; the retrograde date hand and the power-reserve indicator are offered on gold quarter-moon subdials. The watch also offers the delicate chiming of the time via a very refined striking mechanism. This model is water resistant to 30 meters and beats at a rate of 21,600 vibrations per hour.

HARRY WINSTON - OPUS 4

The fourth in Harry Winston's ingenious Opus series of timepieces developed in conjunction with independent watchmakers, the Opus 4 is a true grand complication. Created with Christophe Claret, the master of chiming watches, the Opus 4 is a completely reversible minute-repeater striking on cathedral gongs. One face of the watch reveals the tourbillon and the other features a large moonphase indication with date. The movement, which reverses the direction of the hands for each face, is housed in a platinum Premier case signed by Harry Winston. It is comprised of 423 parts, including 40 jewels, and has 53 hours of power reserve. The Ø 44mm case is water resistant to 30 meters and features a mechanism that allows its reversal. Only 18 platinum Opus 4 watches and two high-jeweled Opus 4 watches will be created.

Multi-Complications

IWC - GRANDE COMPLICATION

This self-winding IWC caliber 79091 (Valjoux 7750 modified base + IWC calendar and repeater modules) offers perpetual calendar (date, day, month, four-digit year, moonphase), minute repeater, and chronograph with three counters. The most impressive complications—perpetual calendar, repeater and chronograph – are combined in this historical watch, a highly valuable timepiece that allows automatic calendar updating until the year 2499; the digits representing 2200 to 2500 are stored in a small glass tube, supplied with the watch. The four-digit year display and the new repeater system with a reduced number of mobile components (some of which have special new designs) are witnesses of a superior class. The Ø 42mm case is waterproof and antimagnetic.

IWC - GRANDE COMPLICATION REF. 3770

This grand complication watch offers chronograph, perpetual calendar, perpetual moonphase indicator, four-digit year indicator, minute repeater and small second with stop device. It houses the caliber 79091 movement with 75 jewels and 44 hours of power reserve. The watch beats at 28,800 vibrations per hour.

ALTERNATE VERSION: 9270 IN PLATINUM WITH PLATINUM BRACELET

Multi-Complications

JAEGER-LECOULTRE - GYROTOURBILLON I

Jaeger-LeCoultre's new patented GyroTourbillon I houses the Caliber 177 complete with a built-in running equation-of-time mechanism, as well as a host of other functions and indications. The exquisite escapement is a first in the history of the tourbillon due to its spherical design, whose multi-dimensional rotation is fascinating, as well as technically advanced. The complex caliber is comprised of 512 parts. In addition to depicting the hours and minutes, its dial also indicates the remaining power reserve, date, month and true solar time as part of the equation-of-time function. The perpetual calendar won't require manual intervention until February 28, 2100. The spherical tourbillon features an aluminum case and an inner titanium and aluminum carriage that is oriented at a 90-degree angle to the outer case, and rotates 2.5 times faster than its companion. The total weight of the nearly 100 components that comprise this spherical wonder is just 0.33 grams.

Grand Complications

PARMIGIANI FLEURIER - TECNICA II

This manual-winding movement (caliber 351, base + calendar module) offers tourbillon, minute repeater and perpetual calendar (date, day, month, four-year cycle). The movement of Tecnica II, with its bridges decorated and beveled by hand, is the sum of three complications and is a unique piece whose complexity matches its rich decoration. Dial and movement—the latter displayed through a wicket hinged on the caseback—are engraved by hand with a drawing representing "Leda in an egg shape" surrounded by the pattern of a square rose, in the spirit of the Art Déco movement of the 1920s and 1930s, dominated by repeated straight lines. Brushed subdials contrast with the dial matted by engravings and the mirror-polished drawings and bevels. The Tecnica II is a unique piece.

Multi-Complications

PARMIGIANI FLEURIER - TECNICA XIV RED FLAMINGO

This unique piece is a manual-winding, 38-jeweled tourbillon that features a minute repeater on two gongs. Beating at 21,600 vibrations per hour, the PF351.02 movement offers 45 hours of power reserve. It also offers perpetual calendar in addition to hour and minute readouts. The Ø 42mm case is crafted in 950 platinum and is double fluted. Water resistant to 30 meters, the Tecnica XIV Red Flamingo features a sapphire crystal and caseback and is entirely hand engraved and decorated. It is covered with translucent red enamel on the caseback and is numbered individually. The hand-engraved dial is 18-karat gold.

PARMIGIANI FLEURIER - TORIC MINUTE REPEATER GMT

The Toric Minute Repeater GMT's manual-winding movement features a minute repeater and dual time readout. The basic movement (Christophe Claret caliber 250 base), finished and adjusted entirely by Parmigiani Fleurier, is integrated by the mechanical components for time indication on a 24-hour basis by an independent hand. The perfection of each technical and aesthetic detail expresses Parmigiani Fleurier's goal to combine the best haute-horology tradition with the best possible improvements. For instance, the hand-decorated details could not have been completed by a machine. Light plays with the small mirrors of polished parts for interesting visual effects.

PARMIGIANI FLEURIER - TORIC WESTMINSTER

The manual-winding movement (caliber 25501, Girard-Perregaux base + second zone module) offers tourbillon, minute repeater and dual time readout. Parmigiani Fleurier added the components for the time indication of a second time zone, which represents an important innovation, to the basic caliber. On the watch's back, the specific components are fastened below the large bridge decorated with a circular graining pattern. The sonnerie strikes the hours and minutes in two different tones, while quarters are indicated by a chime reproducing the famous Westminster melody, played by the clock tower of the London Parliament and now a symbol of England, by four wire gongs tuned to the notes "E-C-D-G" and as many hammers.

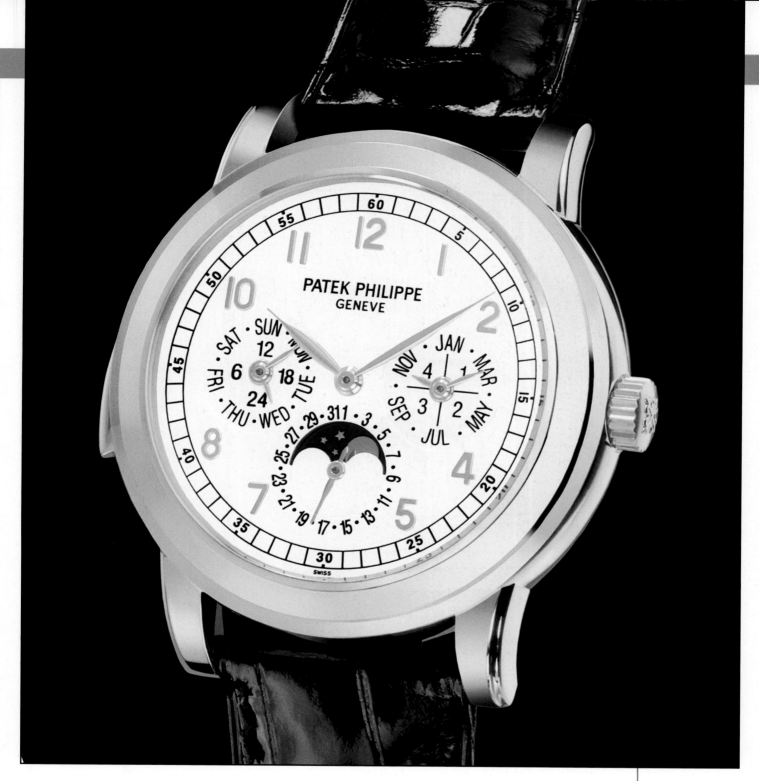

PATEK PHILIPPE - PERPETUAL CALENDAR MINUTE REPEATER REF. 5074

This self-winding, 467-part movement with Geneva Seal (Patek Philippe caliber R 27 Q, R 27 PS base + calendar module) offers perpetual calendar (date, day, month, four-year cycle, moonphase) and minute repeater. The classic Ø 40mm case houses the repeater-perpetual movement realized by Patek Philippe long ago by combining the automatic base including a minute repeater (R 27 PS caliber without seconds) and the most classic calendar module with 24-hour indications. This model, presented in 2001 with the version provided only with the repeater, is meant for a public of connoisseurs. The case size assures a particularly clean and agreeable amplification of the peculiar Cathedral sonnerie. The gong is realized with a special alloy and undergoes several rotations. The full and long-lasting sound thus obtained recalls the bells of ancient cathedrals. The special alloy used for the acoustic gongs, which assures an extraordinary resonance, was developed by Patek Philippe in cooperation with the metallurgy experts of the Federal Swiss Institute of Technology of Lausanne.

Multi-Complications

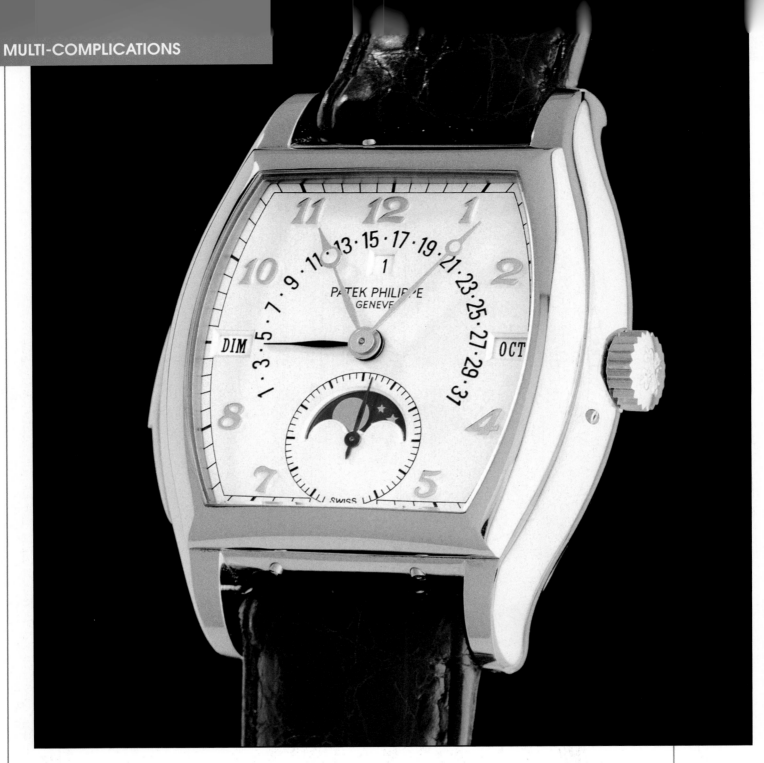

PATEK PHILIPPE - PERPETUAL CALENDAR REPEATER TONNEAU REF. 5013

This self-winding movement with Geneva Seal (Patek Philippe caliber R 27 PS QR, R 27 PS BASE + 126 calendar module) offers perpetual calendar (retrograde date, day, month, four-year cycle, moonphase) and minute repeater. The elegant case in tonneau shape with caseback in sapphire crystal has four small, integrated pushers on its middle for fast calendar correction and a repeater slide as well. The dial shows the analog indications of hour, minute, small second and date (the latter with a retrograde hand), while the day of the week, the month and the four-year cycle are digitally displayed in small windows.

PATEK PHILIPPE - SKY MOON

This self-winding movement with Geneva Seal (caliber 240 CL LU, 240 base + 165 module) offers skymap and moonphase. Without further complications, but provided with the thin 240 automatic movement with its integrated micro-rotor, Patek Philippe's Sky Moon model reproduces the skymap of the sky visible from a certain place (in this piece, the city of Geneva) enclosed in an ellipsis (representing the horizon) on the main dial. It indicates also the positions and sidereal hours of Sirius and the Moon as well as the moonphase in an additional window. These indications are displayed by sapphire discs controlled by a complexity of gears totaling 301 components. The Sky Moon Tourbillon's astronomic mechanism (686 components) is also protected by a patent.

PATEK PHILIPPE - SKY MOON TOURBILLON REF. 5002J

This manual-winding movement with Geneva Seal (Patek Philippe caliber RTO 27 QR SID LU CL) offers tourbillon, minute repeater, perpetual calendar, (retrograde date, day, month, four-year cycle, moonphase) and astronomic functions. On the skymap, the moon (with phases) and the Sirius star indicate their sidereal positions on a 24-hour scale. The sidereal day is determined by two subsequent passages of a star on a meridian (here, the one of Geneva). The sidereal time referred is useful to determine the longitude from a certain place. The ellipsis moves and shows, at any moment, the part of the sky visible from that place (in this case, Geneva). The variations of astronomic indications by few seconds each century are the slightest ones ever obtained by a mechanical watch.

Grand Complications

PATEK PHILIPPE - SPLIT-SECOND CHRONOGRAPH
PERPETUAL CALENDAR REF. 5004

This manual-winding movement (Patek Philippe caliber CHR 27-70 Q, CHR 27-70 base + calendar module) offers perpetual calendar (date, day, month, four-year cycle, moonphase) and split-second chronograph. In 1995, after years of research and development, Patek Philippe's technicians and watchmakers brought one of its most famous complicated wristwatches—realized during the 1950s as Reference 2571—to new life: it is a split-second chronograph with two counters and a perpetual calendar, moonphase indications and a 24-hour display. Its modern descendant, characterized by the digital day and month displays and by the split-second pusher placed on the crown. The gold or platinum case is provided with two backs: one closed and one transparent.

Multi-Complications

PATEK PHILIPPE - STAR CALIBER

Called the Star Caliber, the movement for this watch required eight-plus years in the invention and development stages, houses thousands of tiny parts in a case less than three inches in diameter, and in its finished form costs more than $7 million. The Star Caliber offers 21 different watchmaking complications and six patented inventions. It is the first time in the history of Patek Philippe that one timepieces encases so many patents, including the cherished Westminster Chimes—a sound never fully achieved in a watch until the Star Caliber. The watch chimes the quarter hours and full hours on five separate gongs with remarkable resonance. The watch also chimes the minutes, if the wearer so desires. Additionally, patents are either already granted or pending for the running equation of time, display of sunrise and sunset times, movements of the sky and moon, the selective sprung-cover release mechanism, and the rapid calendar corrector.

Grand Complications

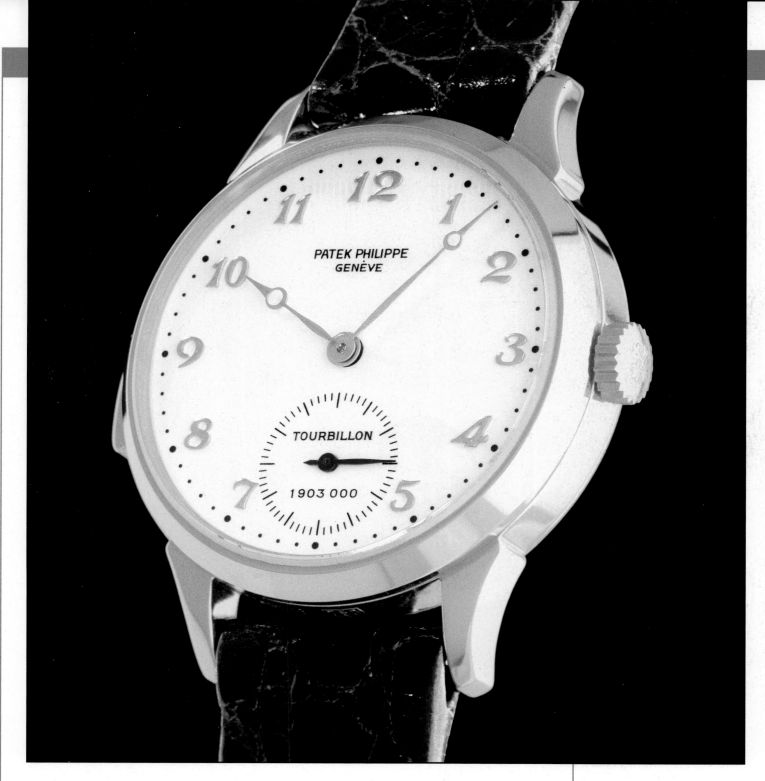

PATEK PHILIPPE - TOURBILLON MINUTE REPEATER REF. 3939 H

Patek Philippe's Tourbillon Minute Repeater's manual-winding movement with Geneva Seal (Patek Philippe caliber RTO 27 PS) features tourbillon and minute repeater. Minute repeaters were among the first complications realized 150 years ago by Patek Philippe, who was the first brand to introduce it in a wristwatch in 1915. A curious feature, common to all the brand's two-hammer repeater watches, is that the maximum number of strokes is totaled at 12:59 with 32 strokes. The movement, equipped with a tourbillon device, is finished to perfection and bears the manufacture's Calatrava cross symbol, which acts as a partial protection of the disconnecting-gear of the repeater device. The dial is genuine enamel.

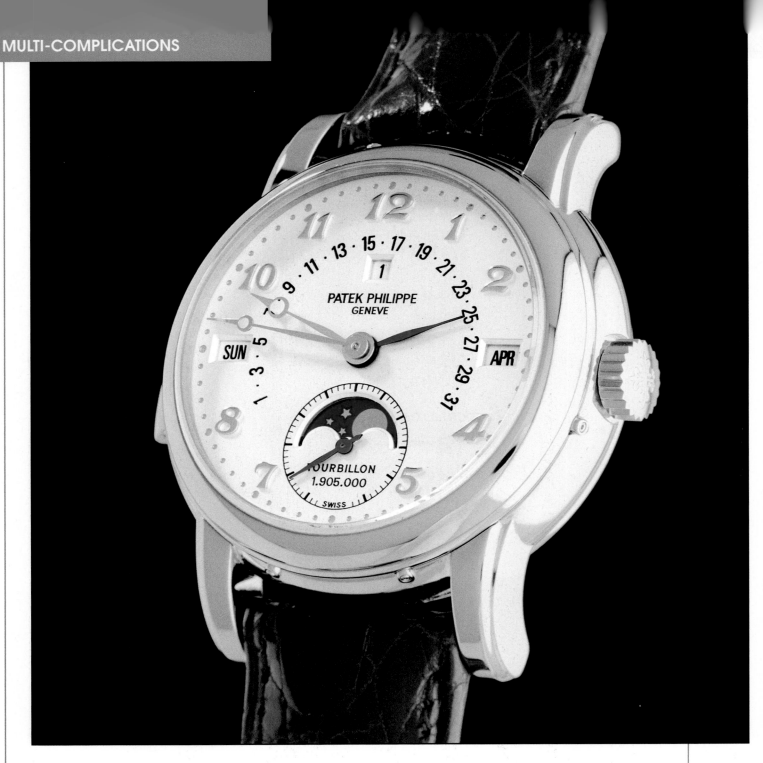

PATEK PHILIPPE - TOURBILLON PERPETUAL CALENDAR REPEATER REF. 5016

This watch's manual-winding movement with Geneva Seal (Patek Philippe caliber RTO 27 PS QR, base + 126 calendar module) offers tourbillon, perpetual calendar (retrograde date, day, month, four-year cycle, moonphase) and minute repeater. For this wristwatch, whose complications are inferior only to the Sky Moon Tourbillon model, Patek Philippe adopted a movement (with a Gyromax balance, as all the Patek watches) provided with a tourbillon device, a perpetual calendar and a minute repeater. Some dial details, such as the lateral calendar windows, remind us of Patek models of the 1930s. The prestigious Geneva Seal, certifying an excellent technical construction and reserved to watches manufactured inside the Canton of Geneva, is engraved on one of the bridges visible through the transparent caseback. The latter is supplied with an additional closed caseback.

ROGER DUBUIS - HOMMAGE CHRONO BI-RETROGRADE
PERPETUAL CALENDAR

This instrument's manual-winding movement with Geneva Seal (Roger Dubuis caliber RD5610, thoroughly modified Lemania base + calendar module) offers perpetual calendar (retrograde date and day, month, four-year cycle, week, moonphase) and chronograph. This watch has six coaxial hands that, starting from the center, give as many indications, two of which appear on a fan-shaped scale. The dial is generous in displaying information and shows a spectacular style. At the center of the dial, the minute counter is positioned at 3:00, month and four-year cycle at 6:00 and continuous seconds at 9:00 cover the rings dedicated to the retrograde day and date indications; the functions are encircled by a 52-week ring.

Multi-Complications

ROGER DUBUIS - SYMPATHIE TOURBILLON BI-RETROGRADE
PERPETUAL CALENDAR

This model's manual-winding movement (Roger Dubuis caliber RD1102, base + calendar module) offers tourbillon and perpetual calendar (retrograde date and day, month, four-year cycle, moonphase). in this model, the perpetual calendar with day and date retrograde hands—a system patented by Roger Dubuis—also includes a tourbillon device, visible through the transparent caseback together with the strongly skeletonized pink-gold bridges. The round dial—perfectly inserted into the unusually shaped square-curved case (water resistant to 3atm)—is characterized by green, blue or totally white mother-of-pearl backgrounds with white inlays.

VACHERON CONSTANTIN - TOUR DE L'ILE

Vacheron Constantin's master watchmakers invested more than 10,000 hours on research and development—almost two years—into this multi-complication. Only seven Tour de L'Ile watches will ever be created and each will house 834 individual parts and offer 16 complications that can be read off of a double-faced watch. The 47mm case houses the new Caliber 2750 with toubillon, minute repeater, moonphase, age of moon, perpetual calendar, second time zone, equation of time, sunrise, sunset, and sky chart. The watch was created in honor of the brand's 250th anniversary, celebrated in 2005.

Multi Complications

TOURBILLONS

One of the most complicated horological complications, the tourbillon (which means "whirlwind" in French) is a highly precise mechanism. The positioning of a watch can cause errors of as much as a second per day and the tourbillon regulator is built to eliminate those errors caused by the force of gravity when the watch is in certain positions.

The constant expansion and contraction of the balance spring in a rigid position causes centrifugal error—when the balance spring dilates on the balance pivot during oscillation while the watch is laid flat. In its vertical position, gravity theoretically cancels out the positional error.

The tourbillon compensates for these differences with its construction, wherein the tourbillon escapement is fitted into a case or carriage and the complete assembly revolves continuously at a constant rate.

A masterpiece of art and technical prowess, the tourbillon was originated by watchmaking legend Abraham-Louis Breguet in 1795, patented in 1801 and marketed in 1805. Indeed, Breguet was a visionary, passionate about measuring and interpreting time in mechanics. Ever the perfectionist, Breguet was obsessed with correcting even the slightest errors in timekeeping.

Prior to the invention of the tourbillon, the escapement and balance spring were mounted rigidly onto the mainplate. Believing this to be the key problem contributing to inaccurate timekeeping, Breguet created a device wherein the balance and escapement are mounted on a movable platform geared to the third wheel. With the repetitive rotation and subsequent averaging effects of gravity over one revolution of the carriage, the resulting errors cancel each other out. Breguet's idea was to make a tourbillon with a one-minute rotation because the seconds' indication on the dial was mounted directly on the carriage pivot, which also rotated once per minute. The entire development process of the tourbillon was an incredible undertaking, one that Breguet executed with equal fortitude. Breguet's invention remains the basis for all tourbillons today.

Other brands followed Breguet and unveiled tourbillon works of art. Girard-Perregaux first unveiled its famed Tourbillon with three gold Bridges in 1867 and the brand has since won numerous awards for other Tourbillon with three gold Bridges models. Similarly, Patek Philippe was also in the forefront of tourbillon mastery. The master house began working on its first tourbillon on October 21,1864 and completed it six months later.

With that creation, Patek Philippe and the tourbillon sparked a romance that has never died. In fact, many of the firm's greatest achievements are its 333 tourbillons that it entered for timing tests at the Geneva Observatory in a 25-year span (from 1943 to 1967).

In 1927, Alfred Helwig unveiled his flying tourbillon regulator (the basis for many of today's flying tourbillons) and Walter Prendel invented a six-minute tourbillon in 1928.

Despite the wide range of advancements in mechanical timekeeping, the tourbillon remains one of the most precise, efficient timekeepers available. Demanding unsurpassed standards of craftsmanship, tourbillons can take as long as six months to produce and usually are created in limited numbers by select watchmakers. In fact, few manufacturers produce tourbillons, and the number of watch companies who utilize the tourbillon movements in their brands' own watches is not significantly higher.

Breguet remains among the masters of tourbillons, joined by such companies as Audemars Piguet, Blancpain, Franck Muller, Girard-Perregaux, IWC, Jaeger-LeCoultre, Jaquet Droz, Parmigiani Fleurier, Roger Dubuis, Richard Mille, Vacheron Constantin and Zenith.

Sometimes these masters combine the tourbillon with one or two other complexities such as perpetual calendars or repeaters. Other times, they combine them with a multitude of complications. For instance, the Opus Four watch (created by Harry Winston in conjunction with Christophe Claret) presents a tourbillon with built-in minute repeater. This reversible masterpiece reveals the tourbillon on one side of the dial and a moonphase on the other.

Tourbillons

Similarly, several of Girard-Perregaux's tourbillons are equipped with additional functions including perpetual calendars and repeaters. In fact, so committed is Girard-Perregaux to perpetuating the art of haute horlogerie that it regularly unveils new tourbillons.

In addition to multiple complexities added to tourbillons, a number of different types of tourbillon regulators exist today. The majority of them have a one-minute rotation, but some have a four-minute rotation and, most recently, Parmigiani Fleurier created a 30-second tourbillon. Additionally, a variety of tourbillon escapement shapes are available. Some have two straight arms, while others have three straight arms, and yet others are even more elaborate.

The exquisite escapement of the tourbillon is a spherical design with incredible multi-dimensional rotation.

Jaeger-LeCoultre has just unveiled the patented, GyroTourbillon I with a built-in running equation-of-time mechanism, as well as a host of other functions and indications. The tourbillon's exquisite escapement is a spherical design with incredible multi-dimensional rotation. The inner titanium cage is positioned at a 90-degree angle to the outer case, and rotates 2.5 times faster than its companion.

Franck Muller's patented Tourbillon Revolution 1 required several years to create and features a mechanism that raises (with the simple push of a button) the tourbillon escapement to the sapphire crystal for better viewing. When the tourbillon's rising function is engaged, the hour and minute hands sweep almost magically to the 12:00 position to make room for the hanging tourbillon case to come to the surface. Now, the Tourbillon Revolution 3 with tri-axial escapement has been released. Indeed, Franck Muller has contributed significantly to the development of the tourbillon and holds 7 patents for its technological developments in this field.

New watchmaking developments and designs are always in the works, but the tourbillon remains a mechanism of fascination and complexity that will forever attract watch collectors.

AUDEMARS PIGUET - CANAPE

The manual-winding Audemars Piguet Caliber 2871 features tourbillon with hour, minute, small second and power reserve. Thanks to its reduced size, the Caliber 2871, consisting of 146 components that are polished and finished by hand, is able to equip the Canapé—whose case is only 23.7mm wide. The dial features an aperture displaying the tourbillon and a power-reserve scale on a guilloché sector.

AUDEMARS PIGUET - EDWARD PIGUET SKELETON TOURBILLON REF. 25947OR

This hand-wound Edward Piguet Skeleton Tourbillon is crafted in 18-karat pink gold with tourbillon regulator and small seconds at 6:00. The rhodium-plated movement is decorated with the Côtes de Genève pattern and circular graining; skeletonized motifs are cut out and engraved by hand. The rectangular case is dedicated to Edward-Auguste Piguet, co–founder of the company. Featuring some of the collection's most elaborate complex auxiliary mechanisms, this product line incorporates a full measure of Audemars Piguet's horological expertise.

AUDEMARS PIGUET - EDWARD PIGUET TOURBILLON

Audemars Piguet has been offering miniaturized tourbillon movements for the wrist for decades. This newest sapphire-backed Edward Piguet Tourbillon with 70 hours of power reserve is created in 18-karat pink or white gold and features a tourbillon aperture at 6:00. It houses the 2878 proprietary hand-wound movement with 177 parts and 21 jewels. The watch beats at 21,600 vibrations per hour and is decorated completely by hand. The bridges are adorned with the Côtes de Genève motif.

AUDEMARS PIGUET - EDWARD PIGUET TOURBILLON REF. 25924PT

This Edward Piguet Tourbillon hand-wound watch is crafted in platinum with tourbillon regulator, and rhodium-plated movement with Côtes de Genève pattern, circular graining and hand engravings. It features a quartz movement mainplate with rutile inclusion. The tourbillon bridge of this Caliber 2888 is inspired by the shape of Galileo's pendulum. Sapphire crystal and caseback.

AUDEMARS PIGUET - EDWARD PIGUET TOURBILLON,

CHRONOGRAPH, POWER RESERVE DYNAMOGRAPH®

The Edward Piguet Tourbillon, Chronograph, Power Reserve Dynamograph® is crafted in platinum with a sapphire caseback. It houses the hand-wound Caliber 2894 with 323 parts and 37 jewels. The watch offers 70 hours of power reserve and features a chronograph with instant jumping minute-counter in titanium. It also houses the Audemars Piguet Dynamograph, or mainspring torque indicator. First unveiled in 2003, the watch features a stunning tourbillon mechanism, visible through a circular aperture at 6:00.

AUDEMARS PIGUET - ROYAL OAK CONCEPT REF. 25980AI

The mechanical manual-winding Royal Oak Concept watch with tourbillon houses the AP Caliber 2896. It offers a power-reserve indicator showing the number of barrel turns (one turn every six hours) and mainspring torque indicator (Dynamograph). The case is alacrite 602 with a titanium bezel and sapphire caseback. It is water resistant and created in a limited edition of 150 pieces.

BLANCPAIN - LEMAN 2100

This self-winding Blancpain caliber 25 (Frédéric Piguet base) offers tourbillon and hour, minute, small second and date readout. The caliber is equipped with a tourbillon volant device provided with a titanium carriage. This original model is presented in only the self-winding version, recently introduced by Frédéric Piguet—who realizes most of the movements used by Blancpain—and with the modern case of the Leman 2100 collection. The dial, characterized by a refined geometry, is dominated by the aperture on the tourbillon and shows the analog indications of date and power reserve.

BLANCPAIN - TOURBILLON GRAND DATE

The Tourbillon Grand Date is housed in an 18-karat rose- or white-gold Léman case. The self-winding watch features a tourbillon aperture at 12:00, and a grand date indicator at 6:00. Additionally, it offers a sapphire caseback displaying the hand-engraved movement and 168 hours of power reserve. The movement, complete with tourbillon escapement, houses 307 individual parts and 35 rubies. Only 50 pieces are being created. The Tourbillon Grand Date is 38mm in diameter, features a sapphire caseback and is water resistant to 100 meters.

BREGUET - CHRONOGRAPH TOURBILLON REF. 3577BA

From the Classique collection, this Chronograph Tourbillon is crafted in 18-karat gold with a fluted case and sapphire caseback. The silvered gold dial is hand-engraved on a rose-engine. It is numbered and holds the Breguet signature. The watch features Roman numerals for the hours and Arabic numerals for the minutes. The tourbillon carriage is at 12:00 and the watch also features a small seconds hand, 30-minute and 12-hour counters. The movement is a hand-wound column-wheel chronograph mechanism with tourbillon. The mechanism is composed of a right-angle lever escapement, a mono-metallic balance wheel with screws, and a compensating balance spring with Breguet overcoil. The one-minute tourbillon with polished steel carriage is driven by the fixed seconds' wheel. The watch is adjusted in six positions and features 25 jewels.

BREGUET - CLASSIQUE REF. 1801

In half-hunter format, this Classique Tourbillon Regulator watch is crafted in 18-karat rose gold. Created in a limited edition of 200 pieces, the Anniversary Tourbillon houses a hand-wound mechanical movement, chased by hand and rhodium plated. The dial for the hours and minutes is at 12:00. The watch features a compensating balance spring with Breguet overcoil and 50 hours of power reserve.

BREGUET - LADY'S CLASSIQUE REF. 3358

This Lady's Classique Grande Complication Tourbillon houses a manual-winding movement with tourbillon and 50 hours of power reserve. Crafted in 18-karat white gold, the watch features a bezel and horns set with 73 diamonds weighing approximately 1.31 carats. The engine-turned dial is mother of pearl.

BREGUET - TOURBILLON REGULATEUR REF. 5307

To create this Classique Tourbillon Regulateur, Breguet developed a new 31-jeweled self-winding movement with an exquisite engine-turned regulator dial. The watch is housed in 18-karat gold with fluted case and sapphire caseback. Water resistant to 30 meters, it features an engine-turned silvered 18-karat gold dial that is individually numbered and signed. There is a secret signature chapter ring with Roman hours at 12:00 and a center minute counter. The tourbillon is at 6:00. The movement, caliber 5587, is an automatic 12-1/2 ligne, 31-jeweled piece that is numbered and signed Breguet. The one-minute tourbillon is hand-engraved and runs off the fixed fourth wheel. The watch offers 120 hours of power reserve from its twin barrels and the hand-engraved rotor is gold. The movement consists of a lateral-lever escapement and balance wheel with adjusting screws on a Breguet spring. The Breguet Tourbillon Regulateur Ref. 5307 is also available in platinum.

CHOPARD - L.U.C 4T QUATTRO TOURBILLON

The L.U.C 4T Quattro Tourbillon from Chopard marks the appearance of the company's first tourbillon. The watch houses the L.U.C 1.02 caliber, which measures 29.1mm in diameter and is 6.1mm thick. It offers 9 hours of power reserve and features the tourbillon escapement, with aperture at 6:00. The carriage completes one full revolution around its axis once per minute. The 224-part L.U.C 1.02 caliber includes the variable inertia four-arm Variner-type balance with integrated inertia blocks. The movement features 33 jewels and beats at a frequency of 28,800 vibrations per hour. The exceptional movement is certified by the Geneva Seal hallmark. The watch is housed in 18-karat rose gold and is water resistant to 30 meters. Only 100 pieces are being created.

DE BETHUNE - CS2

This 18-karat rose-gold timepiece houses a tourbillon, minute repeater, equation of time, and perpetual calendar. The tourbillon is visible through the sapphire caseback, the repeater function is fitted with a strike-silent mechanism and the gongs are tuned with each hammer. The equation of time is measured by the rose-gold center hand and is calculated with the latest astronomic indications. The 319-part manual-winding mechanism houses 20 jewels, a Swiss lever escapement, and Breguet spring balance. The mechanism is decorated with the Côtes de Genève pattern and offers 30 hours of power reserve. The silver dial is hand-guillochéd and features a rose-gold month display at 4:30 and date at 7:30.

FRANCK MULLER - CINTRÉE CURVEX CRAZY HOURS TOURB. REF. 7880 CHT

This Cintrée Curvex Crazy Hours Tourbillon presents an original way of reading the time. The conventional clockwise arrangement of the hours is replaced by a new and original order. The Franck Muller engineers have gone one step further with the Crazy Hours Tourbillon model by combining the Crazy Hours' readout with Franck Muller's hallmark tourbillon. The manual-winding movement beats at 18,000 vibrations per minute, offers 60 hours of power reserve and is comprised of 244 parts and 21 rubies. This watch is available in platinum, 18-karat yellow, white or rose gold, and comes in a variety of dial colors with LumiNova numerals.

FRANCK MULLER - CINTRÉE CURVEX MINUTE REPEATER TOURB. REF. 7880 RMT

Protected by three new patents, the Cintrée Curvex Minute Repeater Tourbillon watch offers hours, minutes and retrograde chime indication. The manual-winding movement is comprised of 371 parts, 32 rubies, beats at 18,000 vibrations per hour and is equipped with 60 hours of power reserve. The watch is available in all three colors of gold and in platinum, as well as in jewelry versions.

FRANCK MULLER - CINTRÉE CURVEX TOURB. REVOLUTION   REF. 7850 T REV 1

This sophisticated model is a flying tourbillon. By pushing the button on the left side of the case, the tourbillon carriage rises up to the level of the sapphire glass and stays there until the pushbutton is released. With this maneuver, the hour and minute hands sweep to 12:00. Upon release of the pushbutton, they fly back to the precise time. Several patents protect this complication. The 299-part manual-winding movement features 70 hours of power reserve, beats at 18,000 vibrations per hour, and is housed in a platinum Cintrée Curvex case.

Grand Complications

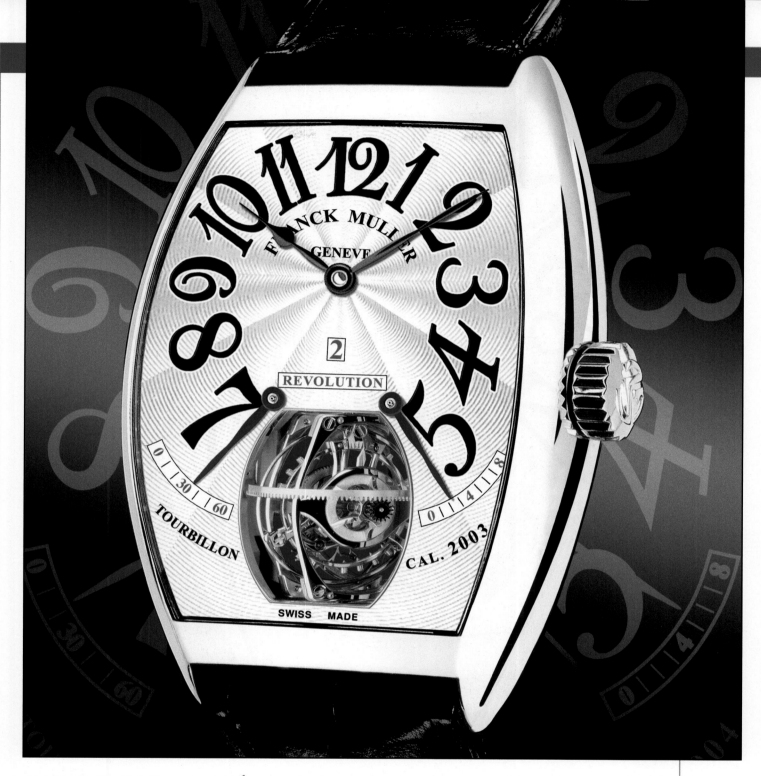

FRANCK MULLER - CINTRÉE CURVEX TOURB. REVOLUTION 2 REF. 7850 T2

The Revolution 2 device is Franck Muller's wristwatch counterpart to the tourbillon pocket watch. Since it was designed for the pocket watch, the classic tourbillon can compensate only for the negative influences of gravity in its vertical position, and the carriage rotates on its single axis. The Revolution 2 revolves around two axes and thereby compensates for the effect of gravity in both the horizontal and vertical positions. The seconds' carriage revolves once every sixty seconds, one minute, the middle carriage once every eight minutes. The 2003 caliber is comprised of 259 parts, including 21 rubies, and offers 70 hours of power reserve.

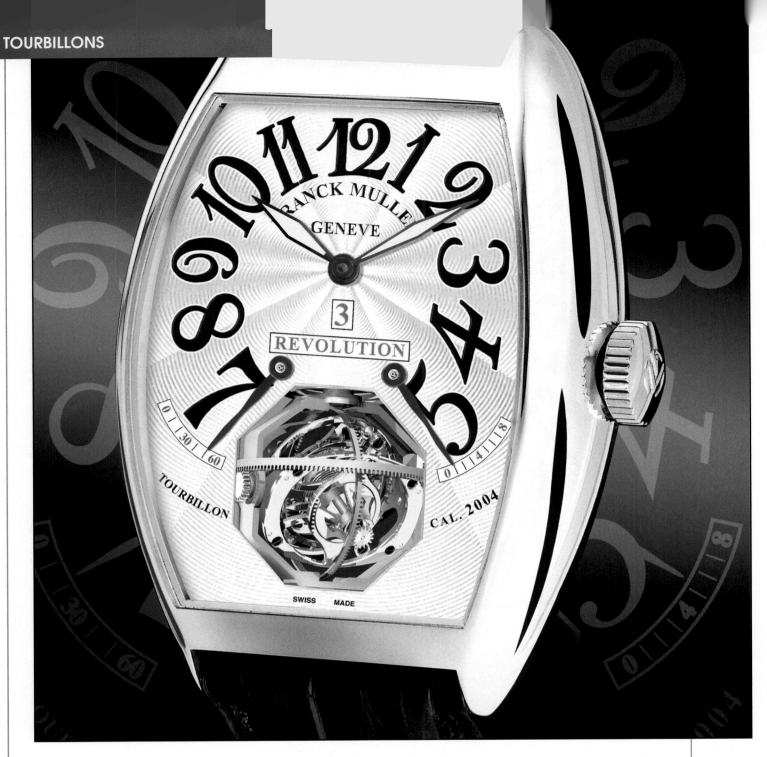

FRANCK MULLER - CINTRÉE CURVEX TOURB. REVOLUTION 3   REF. 98803 T3

This tri-axial tourbillon is housed in a platinum Cintrée Curvex case and is arranged so that the balance wheel and escapement rotating around its axis are contained in Cage A. Cage A is then mounted inside Cage B, so that it can turn about another axis; and Cage B is mounted inside Cage C, which turns about an axis fixed in relation to the timepiece. The seconds' carriage revolves once every 60 seconds, the middle carriage once every eight minutes. The manual-winding 2004 caliber consists of 289 parts and 20 rubies; it offers 10 days of power reserve.

FRANCK MULLER - LONG ISLAND CRAZY HOURS TOURBILLON REF. 1300

This watch represents the first time Franck Muller houses the tourbillon in a Long Island case. The movement is comprised of 244 parts and 21 jewels, and offers 60 hours of power reserve. Available in all colors of gold or in platinum, it features a lacquer-finished dial and decorative filigree figures.

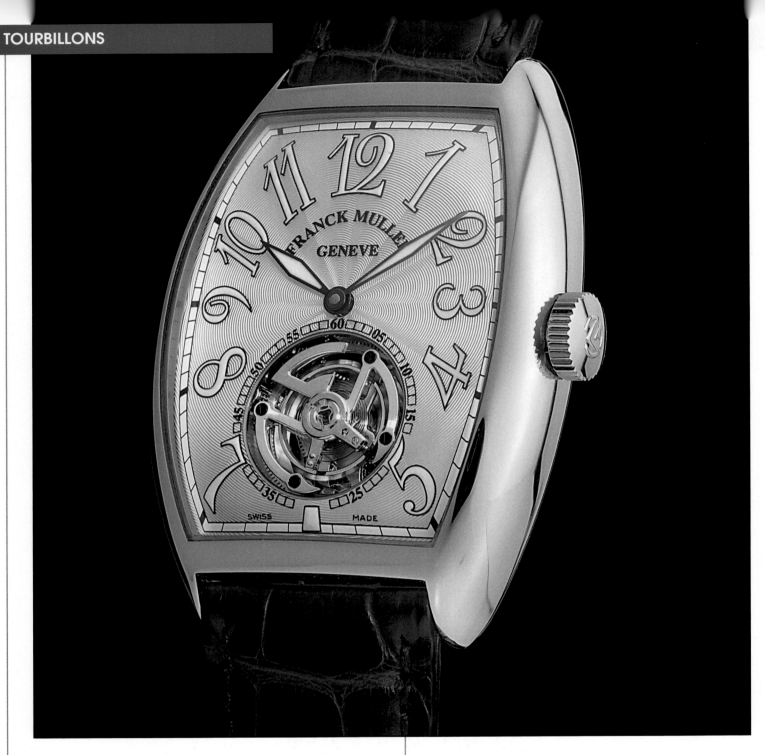

FRANCK MULLER - TOURBILLON VOLANT

Celebrating the brand's 10th anniversary, a tourbillon volant device was introduced into the Cintrée Curvex family. The steel carriage—shaped into Franck Muller's monogram—acted as a catalyzing element with its upper part almost in line with the dial surface. Through the caseback, it is possible to observe the architecture consisting of three separate chased bridges that cover the underlying wheelwork almost completely.

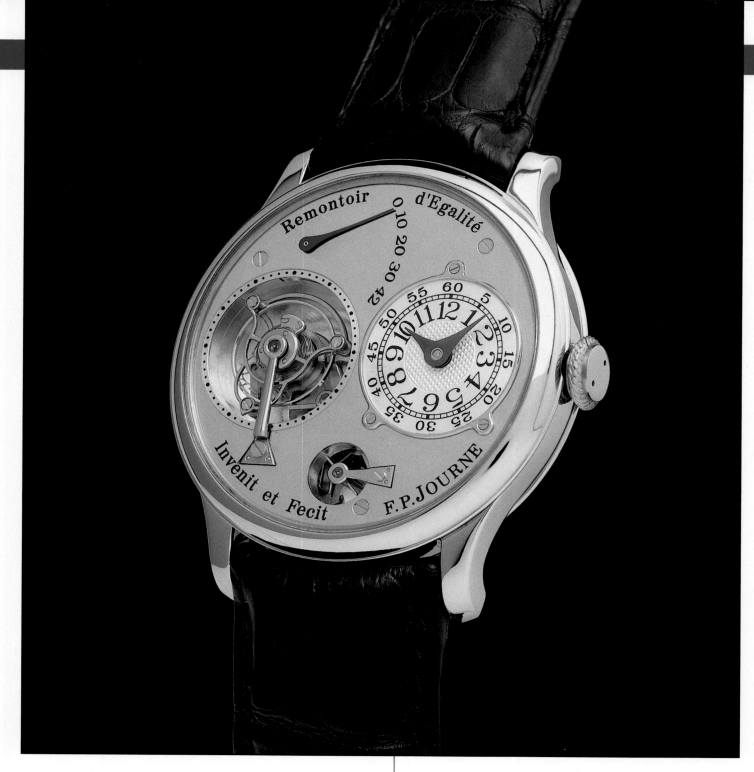

F. P. JOURNE - TOURBILLON SOUVERAIN

This watch's manual-winding F. P. Journe caliber 1498 offers tourbillon and power reserve. The movement, designed and produced by F. P. Journe, avails itself of a remonitoir, or constant device, that is partially visible through the caseback as well as the dial. The constant device is utilized to compensate the difference between the force transmitted by the spring to the escapement, thus improving the synchronization of the balance. The dial features off-center hours; the minutes are displayed on a solid silver guilloché disc locked by a screw-on steel ring fastened to the base.

GÉRALD GENTA - ARENA SPORT TOURBILLON PERPETUAL CALENDAR

From the Arena Sport collection, this Tourbillon Perpetual Calendar watch hosts scintillating subdials and chapter rings on its dial. Crafted in platinum with a palladium bezel, the watch features a perpetual calendar and is equipped with a Gérald Genta tourbillon automatic movement developed internally. The dial offers indications for moonphase, leap years and months, days of the month, small seconds and the days of the week. The movement is coated in antique gold and decorated with a concentric circular graining. The watch has 64 hours of power reserve and is water resistant to 10atm.

GÉRALD GENTA - ARENA SPORT TOURBILLON RETROGRADE HOURS

From the Arena Sport collection, this 41mm watch is offered in platinum with a palladium bezel and a net-like black-and-steel dial. It is equipped with a tourbillon automatic movement developed internally, with a 240-degree retrograde hour, with readout at 12:00. The tourbillon housing is placed at 6:00 and fixed with a sapphire bridge.

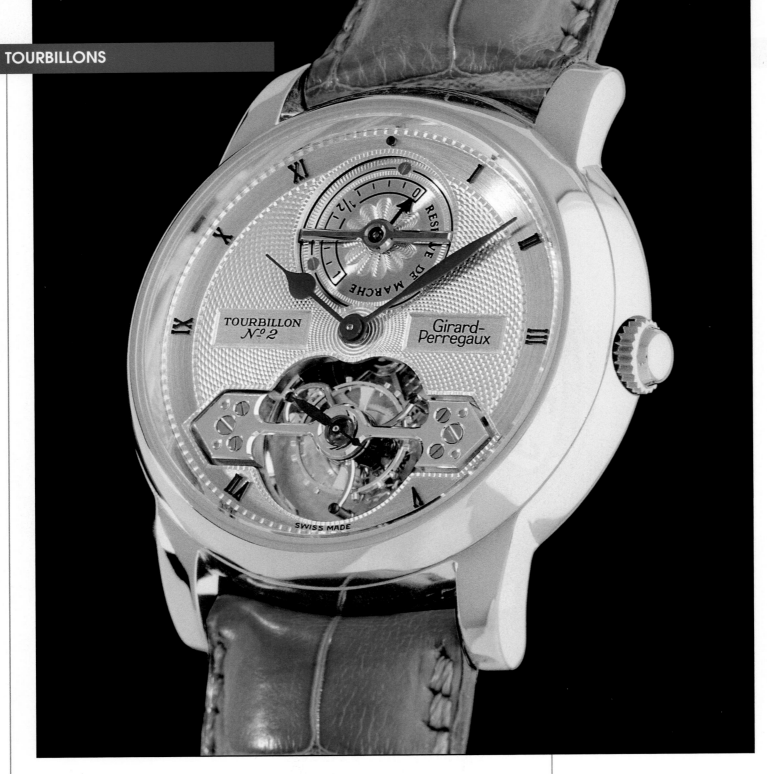

GIRARD-PERRGAUX - TOURBILLON SOUS UN PONT D'OR

One of several versions in the astonishing Tourbillons with gold Bridges series, this model's manual-winding GP 9940 caliber is entirely handmade in-house and has up to 75 hours of power reserve. It is housed in a 38mm yellow-gold case and the motifs—the power-reserve subdial and the opening on the tourbillon complex—fill the solid white-gold and gracefully engine-turned dial.

GIRARD-PERREGAUX - OPERA ONE REF. 99760

Considered a true masterpiece, the Opera One was first released in the year 2000. It features a carillon Westminster, minute repeater, and Tourbillon with three gold Bridges. To increase the mystery and appeal of the Opera One, the watchmakers at Girard-Perregaux revealed the hammers of the striking mechanism and the tourbillon through small apertures on the dial. The magnificent watch houses the manual-winding GP9899 caliber with 75 hours of power reserve.

GIRARD-PERREGAUX - OPERA TWO REF. 99740

The Opera Two features a perpetual calendar in addition to the Opera One's carillon Westminster, minute repeater, and Tourbillon with three gold Bridges. The Opera Two is encased in platinum or pink, yellow, or white gold. Three of the four strike hammers are always visible through the dial and the fourth hammer can be seen when the striking mechanism is operated. The extraordinary complexity of the refined tourbillon movement can be admired through the watch's sapphire caseback. The perpetual calendar indicates the hours and minutes, the day of the week, dates and months, as well as the leap-year cycle. The GP9897 caliber offers 80 hours of power reserve and beats at 21,600 vibrations per hour.

GIRARD-PERREGAUX - PETIT TOURBILLON

This small-size caliber 9700 model (31mm diameter) is among the most fascinating complications of superb mechanical horology available for women. The miniaturization to which the watch had to undergo did not entail any technical modifications and left the prerogatives of its extraordinary quality and beauty—typical for this manual-winding caliber—unchanged. The Petit Tourbillon is available in platinum or any of the three colors of gold. A spectacular version is one studded with diamonds, realized upon request by Girard-Perregaux.

GIRARD-PERREGAUX - RICHEVILLE TOURBILLON W/ GOLD BRIDGE REF. 99310

This Richeville Tourbillon with gold Bridge offers a fluid tonneau shape that is suited to the complication. The tourbillon and pink-gold Bridge can be seen through the cream-colored dial at 6:00. The tourbillon cage is comprised of 72 components and weighs just 0.3 grams—as light as a single swan feather. The movement is the automatic GP9610.T with 30 rubies and beats at a rate of 21,600 vibrations per hour.

Grand Complications

GIRARD-PERREGAUX - TOURBILLON WITH THREE GOLD BRIDGES,
AUTOMATIC SKELETON REF. 99060

Given the prestige of Girard-Perregaux's Tourbillon with three gold Bridges, it is fitting that it should beat at the heart of a stunning skeletonized automatic movement. The watch is crafted in 18-karat gold and features two sapphire crystals to view the movement, which beats at 21,600 vibrations per hour. This watch is water resistant to 30 meters.

Tourbillons

GIRARD-PERREGAUX - TRIBUTE TO ENZO FERRARI TOURBILLON   REF. 99190

The Tribute to Enzo Ferrari Tourbillon with three gold Bridges is created in honor of the new Enzo Ferrari automobile and marks a 10-year alliance between the companies. The Enzo Ferrari Tourbillon is enhanced with a variety of functions, including a chronograph and a perpetual calendar. The watch houses the GP9982 manual-winding movement and offers 70 hours of power reserve. The barrel is decorated with a motif replicating the Enzo's engine. The watch is available in either platinum or 18-karat gold, both with a carbon fiber dial and calendar readout using the same color scheme as the Enzo Ferrari instrument panel. The 43mm case is water resistant to 30 meters.

Grand Complications

GIRARD-PERREGAUX - VINTAGE 1945

This self-winding proprietary caliber 9600 is Girard-Perregaux's smallest Bridge movement. It is realized with only one bridge and housed in the typical rectangular curved case of the Vintage 1945 collection. The self-winding movement with a 45-hour power reserve has a small oscillating mass with a relatively high weight (due to the use of the heavy platinum). The linear cream-colored dial has an aperture on the tourbillon whose rotational motion is displayed under the pink-gold double-arrow bridge.

GIRARD-PERREGAUX - VINTAGE 1945 MAGISTRAL TOURBILLON REF. 99710

Housing the remontage manual-winding GP09700.3950 movement, this stunning Vintage 1945 Magisterial Tourbillon boasts astonishing features that delight both the eye and the ear. The Tourbillon with gold Bridge is visible through the dial aperture at 6:00; the retrograde date hand and the power-reserve indicator are offered on gold quarter-moon subdials. The watch also offers the delicate chiming of the time via a very refined striking mechanism. This model is water resistant to 30 meters and beats at a rate of 21,600 vibrations per hour.

GIRARD-PERREGAUX - VINTAGE 1945 XXL TOURBILLON
PERPETUAL CALENDAR REF. 99860

Housed in the extra-large 18-karat gold Vintage 1945 case, this manual-winding GP9800 caliber watch features a tourbillon and perpetual calendar. The moonphase is at 6:00, thereby leaving no tourbillon aperture on the dial. The month readout is at 12:00, the date is at 3:00, and days of the week are at 9:00. The watch offers 70 hours of power reserve and is water resistant to 30 meters.

GREUBEL FORSEY

The Double Tourbillon 30°—named for the angle that links the two mobile carriages—features a patented double-tourbillon system. Inside a large carriage (which is 15mm in diameter and turns once in a four-minute period) is a second, smaller carriage inclined at a 30-degree angle, revolving once every 60 seconds. This inclination and speed creates the optimal conditions for the balance wheel to oscillate permanently in all positions. Hence, the compensation of the difference in rate due to gravity is no longer limited to the vertical position. The two carriages together contain 128 elements yet weigh only 1.17 grams. The Double Tourbillon 30° is driven by twin barrels, one of which is equipped with a slipping spring to avoid errors caused by excess tension placed on the mechanism during winding. The watch is comprised in total of 301 components, including 39 domed jewels, and has a power reserve of at least 72 hours.

Grand Complications

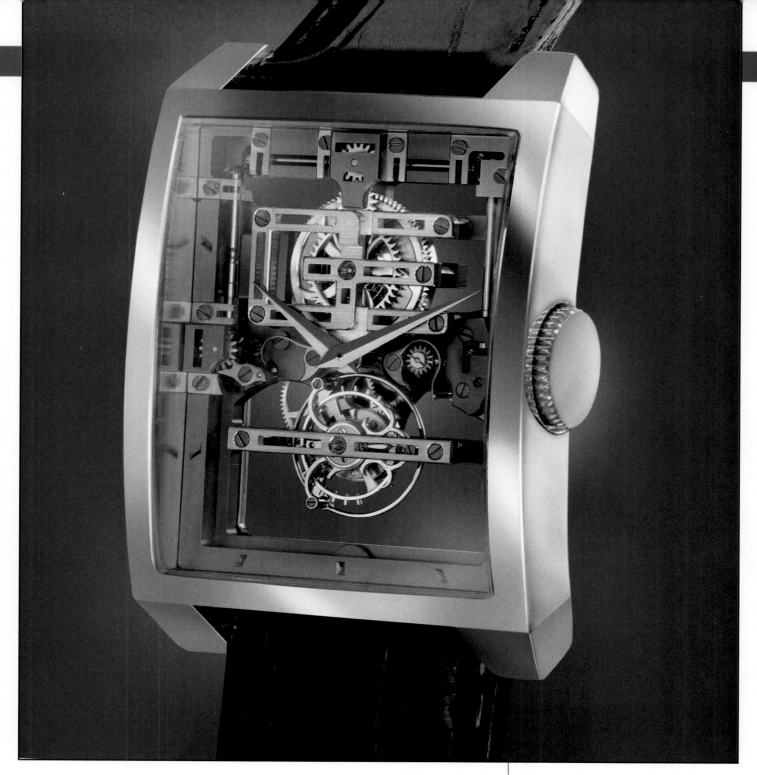

GUY ELLIA - TIME SQUARE Z1 TOURBILLON MAGISTÈRE

A Mystery Tourbillon represents the zenith of the Z1 collection after its recent introduction. This astonishing timepiece was created in collaboration with Christophe Claret, one of the most famous Swiss makers of grand complications and tourbillons. Time Square Z1 features some unique characteristics, such as the essential skeletonized pillar plate with the linear bridges screwed down, symbolizing its creator's initials; an important variation on the traditional Claret winding transmission system, now based on long shafts and 90° bevel gears.

HARRY WINSTON - OPUS 4

The fourth in Harry Winston's ingenious Opus series of timepieces developed in conjunction with independent watchmakers, the Opus 4 is a true grand complication. Created with Christophe Claret, the master of chiming watches, the Opus 4 is a completely reversible minute-repeater striking on cathedral gongs. One face of the watch reveals the tourbillon and the other features a large moonphase indication with date. The movement, which reverses the direction of the hands for each face, is housed in a platinum Premier case signed by Harry Winston. It is comprised of 423 parts, including 40 jewels, and has 53 hours of power reserve. The Ø 44mm case is water resistant to 30 meters and features a mechanism that allows its reversal. Only 18 platinum Opus 4 models and two high-jeweled versions will be created.

IWC - PORTUGUESE TOURBILLON MYSTERE

Housed in the Portuguese case, the Tourbillon Mystere is powered by the IWC automatic movement with seven-day power reserve, the Caliber 50900. The watch features an elevated tourbillon that makes it appear to move freely and entirely independent of any other drive-elements. Only 250 pieces are being created in rose gold and 50 pieces in platinum. This watch offers minute tourbillon, Pellaton automatic-winding mechanism, power-reserve display of 7 days, and small seconds at 9:00.

JAEGER-LECOULTRE - GYROTOURBILLON I

Jaeger-LeCoultre's new patented GyroTourbillon I houses the complex 512-part Caliber 177 complete with a built-in running equation-of-time mechanism, as well as a host of other functions and indications. The exquisite escapement is a first in the history of the tourbillon with respect to its spherical design, whose multi-dimensional rotation is fascinating, as well as technical advancements. In addition to depicting the hours and minutes, the dial also indicates the remaining power reserve, date, month and true solar time as part of the equation-of-time function. The perpetual calendar won't require manual intervention until February 28, 2100. The spherical tourbillon features an aluminum case and an inner titanium and aluminum carriage that is positioned at a 90-degree angle to the outer case, and rotates 2.5 times faster than its companion. The total weight of this spherical wonder is just 0.33 grams.

Grand Complications

JAQUET DROZ - TOURBILLON MINUTE REPEATER

Jaquet Droz's Tourbillon Minute Repeater is crafted in 18-karat white gold and houses a Jaquet Droz 2692.T mechanical movement with a mono-metallic thermally compensated balance wheel. The tourbillon is visible from the caseback and the 43mm watch houses a minute repeater with a strike-to-order on two gongs with two hammers. The movement beats at 18,800 vibrations per hour and features 36 jewels.

PARMIGIANI FLEURIER - FORMA XL 30-SECOND TOURBILLON

This limited edition Forma XL Tourbillon is created in 25 18-karat rose-gold pieces and 25 platinum pieces. The unique tourbillon features a cage with a 30-second rotation, making two complete revolutions in one minute. The watch houses the manual-winding PF500.01 movement with 8 days of power reserve. Beating at 21,600 vibrations per hour, the 28-jeweled movement offers power-reserve indicator and Côtes de Genève decoration. The dial is silvered and finished with a barleycorn guilloché design. The watch is water resistant to 30 meters and features sapphire crystals with antireflection treatment.

PARMIGIANI FLEURIER - TECNICA XIV RED FLAMINGO

This unique piece is a manual-winding, 38-jeweled tourbillon that features a minute repeater on two gongs. Beating at 21,600 vibrations per hour, the PF351.02 movement offers 45 hours of power reserve. It also offers perpetual calendar in addition to hour and minute readouts. The 42mm case is crafted in 950 platinum and is double fluted. Water resistant to 30 meters, it features a sapphire crystal and caseback and is entirely hand engraved and decorated. The Tecnica XIV Red Flamingo's caseback is covered with translucent red enamel and numbered individually. The hand-engraved dial is 18-karat gold.

PARMIGIANI FLEURIER - TORIC

The caliber 28001 (based on the Girard-Perregaux caliber 9900) that equips this model is characterized by bridges decorated with a Côtes de Genève pattern and is mounted, decorated and finished entirely by Parmigiani Fleurier. The barrel jewel becomes a decorative element housed in gold and locked in place by three screws just below the logo at 12:00. The Toric is realized in pink gold or platinum, and also in an exclusive edition with 60 baguette-cut diamonds on the bezel.

PIAGET - EMPERADOR SKELETON TOURBILLON REF. GOA29109

Housing the 600P skeleton mechanical movement with flying tourbillon at 12:00 and 40-hour power reserve indicator at 6:00, this watch beats at 21,600 vibrations per hour. The slimmest shaped tourbillon movement in the world is now incredibly honed, offering only absolutely essential physical proportions. The 42-piece tourbillon carriage weighs scarcely 0.2 grams. From its center radiates the guilloché sunray pattern arranged in 60 zones, representing the seconds or minutes of each rotation. The Piaget Emperador Skeleton Tourbillon is produced in a limited series of just 22 pieces: 11 in pink gold and 11 in white gold.

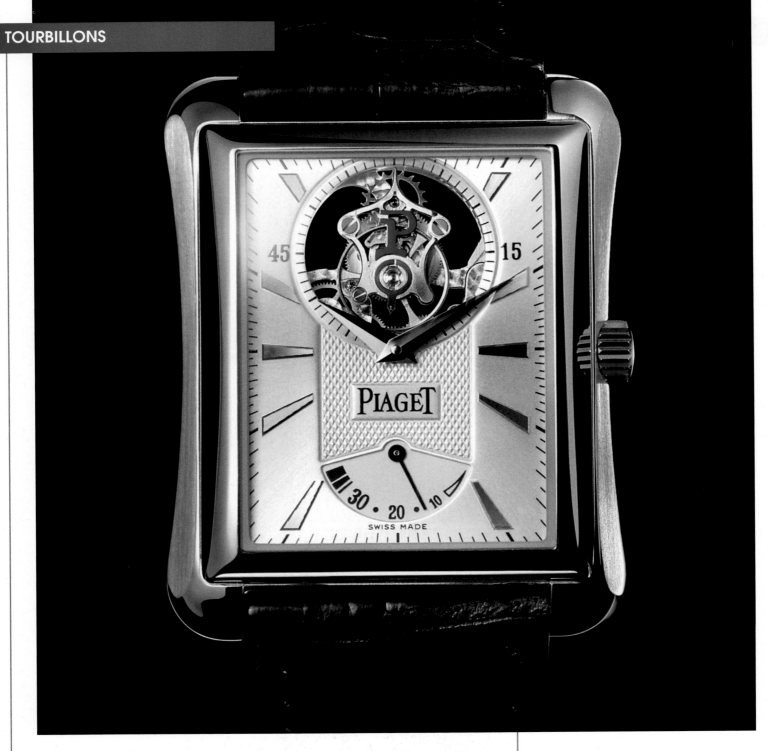

PIAGET - EMPERADOR TOURBILLON REF. GOA28074

Designed, developed and produced at the La Côte-aux-Fées manufacture, this new Piaget movement is a symbol of technical prowess. The watch houses the 600P mechanical tourbillon movement with 40 hours of power reserve. It beats at a rate of 21,600 vibrations per hour and houses 24 jewels. It is perfectly in line with the Piaget lineage of extra-slim calibers,for which the brand is highly regarded. With a thickness of only 3.5mm, this caliber is the slimmest shaped tourbillon movement in the world. From the earliest stages of its development, it was designed to fit into the curved rectangular Emperador watchcase. For this watch, Piaget selected a flying tourbillon: suspended by a single arbor, the cage is displayed through an aperture at 12:00. The dial, the center of which is engraved with pointed barleycorn guilloché, is enhanced by 10 gold applique indexes. The crystal and transparent caseback are sapphire. The three bridges of the tourbillon cage are made of titanium, comprising 42 components and making one revolution per minute.

Grand Complications

PIAGET - POLO TOURBILLON REF. GOA29064

In celebration of the Polo collection's 25th anniversary, Piaget offers the bejeweled Piaget Polo Tourbillon. The entirely gemset timepiece (with 759 diamonds weighing nearly 61 carats) houses the exquisite mechanical 600P flying-tourbillon movement. The shaped movement is just 3.5mm thick, the slimmest in the world. It incorporates 24 rubies and offers 40 hours of power reserve. The tourbillon's bridges are crafted in titanium and the watch is set with trapeze and baguette-cut diamonds. In addition to the diamond-bedecked dial, case, caseback and bracelet, the tourbillon aperture and the power-reserve indicator on the dial are outlined with 40 sapphires.

PIERRE KUNZ - TOURBILLON VOLANT

An identifying feature of the Pierre Kunz collection is masculine cases housing calibers with flyback indications. This manual PKA 3201 offers a flying tourbillon through the dial at 6:00 and the retrograde day-date, adjustable via two small pushers on the middle. White or pink18-karat gold enriches the typical oversized Pierre Kunz case with cannelé middle and brushed bezel. A sapphire-crystal caseback is held by six screws and reveals the movement's bridges, smoothly decorated with a Cotes de Genève pattern.

RICHARD MILLE - RM 002 TOURBILLON

The RM 002 Tourbillon—an evolution of the first Richard Mille timepiece—houses the hand-wound RM 002 Caliber with hour, minute, 70 hours of power reserve and torque indicator. The torque indicator shows the main spring tension and enables the movement timing to be optimized. The watch also features a variable inertia balance for better reliability in the event of shock. The watch features a titanium movement plate and a ceramic counter pivot. It is crafted in the signature three-piece Richard Mille case with sapphire caseback. Water resistant to 50 meters, this watch is crafted in platinum, titanium, or in white or pink gold.

RICHARD MILLE - RM 003 TOURBILLON

The RM 003 Tourbillon Double Fusee houses the mechanical manual-winding movement with splined screws in grade 5 titanium for the bridges and case to permit better control of the screw torque. The watch, which consists of a tourbillon, second time-zone indicator and torque indicator, hosts 23 jewels and beats at a rate of 21,600 vibrations per hour. The end stone of the tourbillon cage is made of ceramic and the pushbutton at the center of the crown allows for three functions to be selected simply by pressing it: winding; time-setting; neutral.

RICHARD MILLE - RM 006 TOURBILLON

The first watch to be designed with a carbon fiber movement plate, this RM 006 Tourbillon required years to develop. The manual-winding watch with hour and minute indicators and power reserve of 48 hours has a composite plate made of carbon nano-fibers. It is cast under a high-compression system that creates an isotope, giving physical and chemical mechanical stability to the whole watch. The spline screws are titanium and the case is either titanium, or white or pink gold. The watch houses 19 jewels and beats at a rate of 21,600 vibrations per hour. Shown is one of 20 pieces with a carbon fiber movement plate.

RICHARD MILLE - RM 008 TOURBILLON CHRONOGRAPH

Housing a manual-winding mechanism, this watch offers hour, minute, 70 hours of power reserve, torque indicator, split-second chronograph and function indicator. The column-wheel chronograph is crafted of titanium, and is operated by pressing the pusher at 8:00. The watch features a variable inertia balance wheel and a fast-rotating barrel (6 hours per revolution instead of 7.5 hours). It features a bottom plate and center bridge of titanium. The RM 008 Tourbillon Chronograph is offered in titanium or gold.

RICHARD MILLE - RM 009 TOURBILLON

The revolutionary RM 009 tourbillon features a bottom plate in aluminum-lithium. The case is made of Aluminum AS7G-Silicium-Carbon (ALUSIC), an extremely exclusive material reserved solely for use in satellites, due to its enormous cost. Its main characteritics are a superior level of rigidity, a high resistance to wear. Its density of 2.95 allows the total watch head (case and movement) to weight less than 30 grams, making it by far the lightest mechanical watch ever made.

ROGER DUBUIS - COLLECTION GOLDENSQUARE TOURBILLON

REF. G40 03 5 GN1.7A

This 28-piece limited edition 40mm GoldenSquare Tourbillon with mother-of-pearl dial houses the RD 03 caliber mechanical manual-winding movement with 15 lines and 27 jewels. The movement is rhodium plated and decorated with the Côtes de Genève pattern. Adjusted in five positions, the watch houses a flying tourbillon with instantaneous date and power-reserve indicator. The tourbillon carriage is visible at 7:00.

ULYSSE NARDIN - FREAK CAROUSEL

Nothing quite like the Freak Carousel has ever been seen in the field of horology. Its entire movement turns with the carriage, regulating organ and escapement. The winding spring occupies the entire available surface and assures 8 days of autonomy. The hands are cut from the bridges. The unusual Dual-Direct escapement has two wheels provided with a ceramic layer, a material that does not require lubrication. Time is set from the bezel and winding is performed from the caseback.

VACHERON CONSTANTIN - MALTE TOURBILLON REF. 30067

Housed in a stunning 18-karat pink-gold tonneau case, this Malte Tourbillon is powered by the hand-wound 1790 mechanical caliber with tourbillon regulator. It offers a 31-day analog date calendar, 55 hours of power reserve. and is completely open-worked and beveled.The dial features baton hands and a crown signed with the embossed symbol of Vacheron Constantin.

VACHERON CONSTANTIN - SAINT-GERVAIS

This complicated watch pushes the existing limits of the power reserve. A world-first with four barrels coupled with a regulator tourbillon and a perpetual calendar, the watch has 250 hours of power reserve. The 44mm platinum-cased timepiece houses the new Caliber 2250 with 410 parts. In addition to the gold hour and minute hands, two blued steel hands run over the silvered engine-turned gold dial in arcs at 3:00 and 9:00 to indicate the power reserve of the barrels. Only 55 pieces of this watch will be created.

ZENITH - GRANDE CHRONOMASTER XXT TOURBILLON

After three years of research and development, Zenith releases the Grande ChronoMaster XXT Tourbillon. Housing the famed El Primero movement with chronograph that beats at a record 36,000 vibrations per hour, the watch also features a patented calendar disc that is inserted between the bridge and the tourbillon carriage, turning in the opposite direction. This new movement, the caliber 4005, consists of 310 parts. The dial is strikingly clean considering the number of functions the watch has to offer: tourbillon, date, 12-hour, 30-minute, and center hour, minute and second.

ZENITH - STAR TOURBILLON EL PRIMERO

This Star Tourbillon houses the bidirectional automatic chronograph movement with tourbillon, El Primero 4029.The 14 1/4''' caliber is Ø 32x7.55 high with 292 parts, 36,000 vph, 50+ hours of power reserve, 35 jewels, central rotor on ball bearings, and measures to 1/10th of a second. Water resistant to 30 meters, the 18-karat white-gold case, bezel and horns are set with 117 baguette-cut diamonds (8.79 carats), 18-karat white-gold Zenith pushbuttons and crown are set with a Star diamond. The case is Ø 40mm with a Ø 32mm opening. Curved, sapphire crystal is antireflective on both sides, caseback also is transparent sapphire crystal. White-gold and mother-of-pearl dial is set with 112 diamonds (0.292 carat), a Zenith Star in diamond (0.5 carat) overhangs the tourbillon bridge. Two Zenith Stars symbolize the 30-minute and 12-hour counters. Watch mounted on black satin strap with 18-karat white-gold Star triple-folding buckle stamped with Zenith Star.

MINUTE REPEATERS AND SONNERIES

Arguably the most beautiful of all complications are the

minute repeaters and sonneries. These exceptional

watches house not only hundreds of tiny

pieces, including miniature

hammers and gongs, but

also—and most

importantly—chime

the time with beautiful,

unrivaled melodious

sounds.

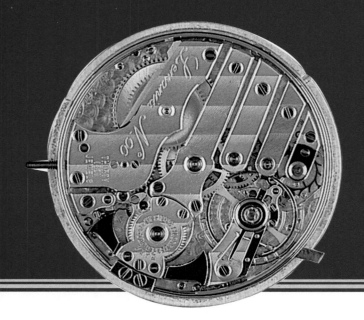

Essentially, a repeater houses a striking mechanism activated by the wearer. With the push of a button or the move of a slide, the time is chimed via different tones, thanks to a very complex mechanical device. Employing a similar system, but without needing to be activated by the wearer, are sonneries.

There are quarter repeaters (in which the last hour and the quarter hour are indicated using two differently pitched tones) and minute repeaters (in which the hour, quarter-hour and minutes are sounded). Additionally, albeit a bit more rare, there are half-quarter repeaters (in which the hour, quarters and nearest half quarter-hours are sounded), and five-minute repeaters (in which the last hour, the quarters and one strike for each five minutes past the last quarter are sounded). As a result of different hammers striking gongs in contrasting reverberations, each strike of hours, quarters and minutes has its own distinct sound.

The sonnerie is another type of repeater that strikes the hours and quarter hours regularly without the wearer needing to press a button. Also known as "strikes," these watches can be found in grande strikes or sonneries that chime the hours and the quarters, and petit strikes or sonneries that chime only the hours.

Chiming watches' roots were planted firmly nearly a century ago. The initial mechanism utilized in sonneries and repeaters is derived from the chiming systems of clock towers of

the 14th and 15th centuries. Indeed, watch books reference the Visconti Palace in Milan in 1335, wherein a large clock with a clapper strikes 24 times over the course of a day and night to indicate the hours.

The system was not perfected for table clocks until about 1687, when English watchmaker Daniel Quare succeeded in applying a repeater mechanism to smaller timekeepers. By utilizing this chiming system in clocks in the home, owners could learn the time at any hour of the day or night without having to light a candle or oil lamp. Early repeating clocks sounded the time via a bell attached to the back of the case. However, this changed in the late 18th century when the esteemed Abraham-Louis Breguet (credited as the father of modern repeating watches) invented a gong spring in 1783. Essentially, Breguet replaced the traditional bell with a strip spring wrapped around the movement. This invention improved sound quality and reduced awkwardness and the size of a timepiece.

Today, the finest watchmakers create repeaters and sonneries of all types. Most often, they are ensconced in diamonds and gemstones so that the beauty of the outer case matches the melodious perfection inside. In fact, several years ago Audemars Piguet embellished its repeater complication with nearly 500 diamonds and emeralds weighing 50 carats.

Additionally, the finest watchmakers constantly fine-tune the chimes and sounds of their gongs, often offering more elaborate striking systems. Several are even turning to Westminster chimes for their beautiful tunes. Others work to miniaturize the movements. Jaeger-LeCoultre, for instance, not only miniaturized the system, but developed an entirely new one to fit into a rectangular caliber (the caliber 943), enabling it to create the Reverso Repetition minutes.

Other advances in minute repeaters come in the form of new slide mechanisms, improving all-or-nothing striking, silencers, and new metallurgical acoustic combinations.

AUDEMARS PIGUET - JULES AUDEMARS DYNAMOGRAPH

This Jules Audemars Dynamograph with chiming grand strike and power reserve houses the manual-winding Caliber 2891. A totally original feature that Audemars Piguet first presented in 2000, the Dynamograph provides real-time indication of the mainspring's winding stress. In this grand-strike repeater watch, Audemars Piguet added the Dynamograph readout for the first time. The watch is crafted in 18-karat white gold.

AUDEMARS PIGUET - JULES AUDEMARS GRANDE COMPLICATION REF. 258660R

The elegant Jules Audemars Grande Complication houses the self-winding Caliber 2885 with more than 600 components. The watch offers perpetual calendar, minute repeater, and split-second chronograph. It is housed in 18-karat pink gold and features five correctors and a slide for the repeater on the side. The month and four-year cycle are at 6:00 and the moonphase and date are at 12:00. This watch is also available in platinum.

BOVET - TOURBILLON MINUTE REPEATER

This majestic inverted Tourbillon Minute Repeater is crafted in platinum. The hand-wound watch features an upside-down movement, wherein the chiming work of the repeaters, as well as the tourbillon and going train, are under the dial. Essentially, the drive of the movement has been reversed so that the hands turn properly on the dial. This invention enables the mechanism to be displayed in new ways on the watch face. The dial is cut away to show the tourbillon carriage flanked by the engraved bridges of the movement, with the under-dial mechanism being held by a bridge on top of the dial. This watch houses a 39-jeweled, 18,000 vibrations-per-hour movement inside a 39mm Bovet Fleurier case. Only 12 of these movements will be made per year.

BVLGARI - ANFITEATRO RÉPÉTITION MINUTE

Introducing the Anfiteatro Tourbillon and the Anfiteatro Répétition Minute, Bvlgari signaled its jump to the great complications with Girard-Perregaux as its movement consultant and supplier. The Minute Repeater's platinum case houses the 9950 caliber, one of the most reliable movements based on a manual Lemania 399 with Girard-Perregaux modifications. Some other features include the crown and the slide in white gold, the back with a sapphire glass, open to reveal the magnificent movement held by eight small white-gold screws; the argenté dial covers its solid gold base.

DE BETHUNE - CS2

This 18-karat rose-gold timepiece is a masterful work of horological tradition. It houses a tourbillon, minute repeater, equation of time, and perpetual calendar. The tourbillon is visible through the sapphire caseback. The repeater function is fitted with a strike-silent mechanism and the gongs are tuned with each hammer. The equation of time is measured by the rose-gold center hand and is calculated with the latest astronomic indications. The 319-part manual-winding mechanism houses 20 jewels, a Swiss lever escapement, and Breguet spring balance. The mechanism is decorated with the Côtes de Genève pattern and offers 30 hours of power reserve. The silver dial is hand-guillochéd and features a rose-gold month display at 4:30 and date at 7:30

DE BETHUNE - MINUTE REPEATER, PERPETUAL CALENDAR CS3

This one-of-a-kind Minute Repeater, Perpetual Calendar CS3 watch offers moonphase indicator on a second dial (not shown). The platinum-cased watch features a minute repeater with a strike-silent mechanism, and gongs that are tuned with each hammer for high-quality sound. Its perpetual calendar is equipped with moonphase indication, month at 3:00, date at 6:00, and day at 9:00. The 42mm case features the slide repeater at 10:00, octagonal crown and sapphire caseback. The 301-part movement is a Swiss lever escapement caliber with 20 jewels and Breguet balance spring. It beats at 18,000 vibrations per hour and offers 24 hours of power reserve. Winding and time-setting functions are adjusted through the crown in two positions. All steel components are polished and hand decorated with the Côtes de Genève pattern.

DE BETHUNE - MONO-PUSHER MINUTE REPEATER CS4

An unusual watchmaking feat, the Mono-Pusher Minute Repeater is the first to be equipped with a strike-silent mechanism via a simple press on the crown. The repeater function is equipped with an independent wheels system, armed by the crown, which allows for the watch's water resistance. The gongs of the striking are tuned with each hammer and the high quality of the mechanism gives high precision to the striking. The movement is entirely hand-guillochéd with a DE BETHUNE décor. The 42mm case is crafted in rose gold, and features a silver-plated gold dial with hand-guillochéd pattern. The 266-part manual-winding movement beats at 21,600 vibrations per hour and offers 24 hours of power reserve.

de GRISOGONO - OCCHIO RIPETIZIONE MINUTI REF. N0 1

The Occhio Minute Repeater strikes the minute, quarter-hour and hour on three Cathedral gongs with a retracting twelve-blade, matte black ceramic diaphragm. This limited 50-piece edition is water resistant to 30 meters and crafted in blackened white gold and platinum on a black genuine alligator strap with white-gold de GRISOGONO folding clasp. The Arabic numerals are in silvered script and the Dauphine-style hands are white gold.

de GRISOGONO - OCCHIO RIPETIZIONE MINUTI REF. N0 2

The Occhio Minute Repeater strikes the minute, quarter-hour and hour on three Cathedral gongs with a retracting twelve-blade, matte black ceramic diaphragm. This limited 50-piece edition is water resistant to 30 meters and crafted in pink gold and platinum on a black genuine alligator strap with pink-gold de GRISOGONO folding clasp. The Arabic numerals are in red gilt script and the Dauphine-style hands are pink gold.

FRANCK MULLER - CINTRÉE CURVEX MINUTE REPEATER
TOURBILLON 7880 RMT

Protected by three new patents, the Cintrée Curvex Minute Repeater Tourbillon watch offers hours, minutes and retrograde chime indication. The manual-winding movement is equipped with 60 hours of power reserve. The watch is available in all three colors of gold and platinum, as well as in jewelry versions. The movement is comprised of 371 parts, 32 rubies and beats at 18,000 vibrations per hour.

GÉRALD GENTA - OCTO GRANDE SONNERIE

This manual-winding caliber GG 31000 offers tourbillon, grand and petite sonneries, minute repeater and double power reserve. The Grande Sonnerie model, presented for the first time in 1994, was reworked for this new version for the 30th anniversary of the Gérald Genta brand. The very limited space of this wristwatch's movement with off-center hour display, tourbillon and two barrels also houses the repeater mechanisms and the "au passage" strike-work with a four-hammer Westminster chime. On the caseback, there are subdials for the power reserve (movement and sonnerie) and for the sonnerie mode selection (grande, petite, mute).

GIRARD-PERREGAUX - OPERA ONE REF. 99760

Considered a true masterpiece, the Opera One was first released in the year 2000. It features a carillon Westminster, minute repeater, and Tourbillon with three gold Bridges. To increase the mystery and appeal of the Opera One, the watchmakers at Girard-Perregaux revealed the hammers of the striking mechanism and the tourbillon through small apertures on the dial. The Opera One houses the manual-winding GP9899 caliber with 75 hours of power reserve.

GIRARD-PERREGAUX - OPERA TWO REF. 99740

The Opera Two features a perpetual calendar in addition to the carillon Westminster, minute repeater, and Tourbillon with three gold Bridges. The Opera Two is housed in a case of pink, yellow, or white gold, or in platinum. Three of the four strike hammers are visible through the dial. The fourth hammer can be seen only when the striking mechanism is operated. The extraordinary complexity of the refined tourbillon movement can be admired through the watch's sapphire caseback. The perpetual calendar indicates the hours and minutes, the day of the week, dates and months, as well as the leap-year cycle. The GP9897 caliber offers 80 hours of power reserve, and beats at 21,600 vibrations per hour.

GIRARD-PERREGAUX - VINTAGE 1945 MAGISTRAL TOURBILLON REF. 99710

Housing the remontage manual-winding GP09700.3950 movement, this stunning Vintage 1945 Magistral Tourbillon boasts astonishing features that delight both the eye and the ear. The Tourbillon with gold Bridge is visible through the dial aperture at 6:00; the retrograde date hand and the power-reserve indicator are offered on gold quarter-moon subdials. The watch also offers the delicate chiming of the time via a very refined striking mechanism. This model is water resistant to 30 meters and beats at a rate of 21,600 vibrations per hour.

HARRY WINSTON - OPUS 4

The fourth in Harry Winston's ingenious Opus series of timepieces developed in conjunction with independent watchmakers, the Opus 4 is a true grand complication. Created with Christophe Claret, the master of chiming watches, the Opus 4 is a completely reversible minute-repeater striking on cathedral gongs. One face of the watch reveals the tourbillon and the other features a large moonphase indication with date. The movement, which reverses the direction of the hands for each face, is housed in a platinum Premier case signed by Harry Winston. It is comprised of 423 parts, including 40 jewels, and has 53 hours of power reserve. The Ø 44mm case is water resistant to 30 meters and features a mechanism that allows its reversal. Only 18 platinum Opus 4 watches and two high-jeweled Opus 4 watches will be created.

IWC - GRANDE COMPLICATION REF. 3770

This grand complication watch offers chronograph, perpetual calendar, perpetual moonphase indicator, four-digit year indicator, minute repeater and small second with stop device. It houses the caliber 79091 movement with 75 jewels and 44 hours of power reserve. The watch beats at 28,800 vibrations per hour.

ALTERNATE VERSION: 9270 IN PLATINUM WITH PLATINUM BRACELET.

IWC PORTUGUESE MINUTE REPEATER REF. 5240

This Portuguese Minute Repeater houses the 95290 caliber with 54 rubies and beating at 18,000 vibrations per hour. It offers 43 hours of power reserve and features a stunning minute repeater function with small second and stop device. It is offered in limited editions of platinum and all three colors of gold.

IWC - PORTUGUESE MINUTE REPEATER SQUELETTE REF. 5241

Technically and aesthetically advanced, this stunning Portuguese watch houses the mechanical minute-repeater movement 95911 with Breguet spring. It houses 54 jewels and offer 43 hours of power reserve. The skeletonized watch even displays the hammer through its sapphire crystals. The case is 42mm in diameter.

JAQUET DROZ - TOURBILLON MINUTE REPEATER

Jaquet Droz's Tourbillon Minute Repeater is crafted in 18-karat white gold and houses a Jaquet Droz 2692.T mechanical movement with a mono-metallic thermally compensated balance wheel. The tourbillon is visible from the caseback and the 43mm watch houses a minute repeater with a strike-to-order on two gongs with two hammers. The movement beats at 18,800 vibrations per hour and features 36 jewels.

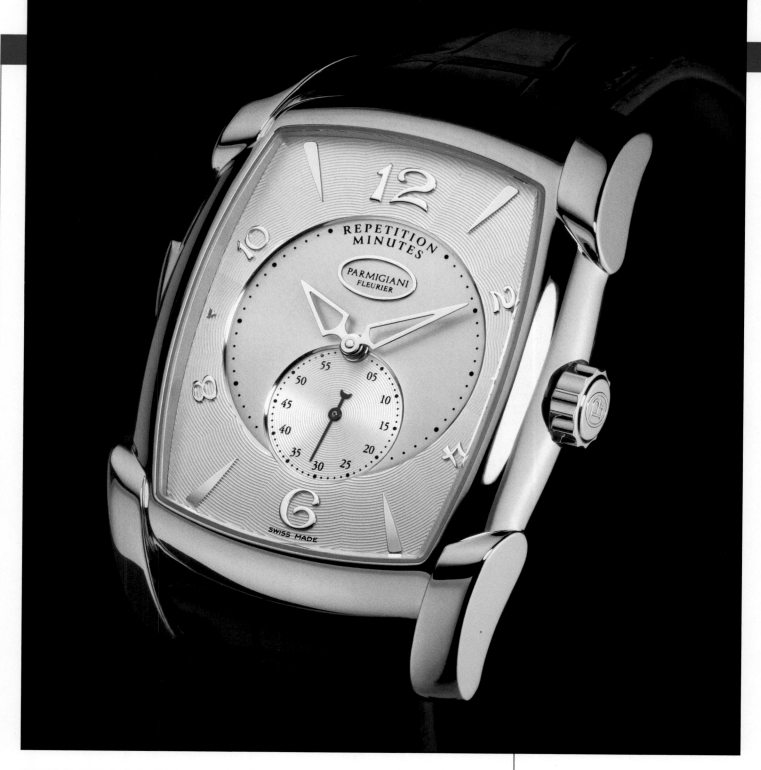

PARMIGIANI FLEURIER - FORMA XL MINUTE REPEATER

Housing the PF350.01 manual-winding movement, this Forma XL Minute Repeater strikes the hours, quarter-hours and minutes on two gongs. The watch offers a power reserve of 45 hours and beats at 21,600 vibrations per hour. The 33-jeweled movement features the Côtes de Genève decoration and hand-chamfered bridges. Crafted in 18-karat rose gold or in platinum, the watch features a guilloché dial and applied Arabic numerals. Through the caseback, one can view the two small sapphire crystals beneath the hammers. Each watch is individually numbered on the back.

PARMIGIANI FLEURIER - TECNICA XIV RED FLAMINGO

This unique piece is a manual-winding, 38-jeweled tourbillon that features a minute repeater on two gongs. Beating at 21,600 vibrations per hour, the PF351.02 movement offers 45 hours of power reserve. It also offers perpetual calendar in addition to hour and minute readouts. The 42mm case is crafted in 950 platinum and is double fluted. Water resistant to 30 meters, it features a sapphire crystal and caseback and is entirely hand engraved and decorated. The Tecnica XIV Red Flamingo's caseback is covered with translucent red enamel and numbered individually. The hand-engraved dial is 18-karat gold.

PARMIGIANI FLEURIER - TORIC

This manual-winding caliber.P.F. 250, (Christophe Claret base) houses the minute repeater. Platinum and yellow gold are used on request. The slate-gray dial is guilloché with a barley-grain pattern and provided with Javeline hands. The basic caliber, whose bridges are redesigned, was thoroughly modified by the house specifically to meet the quality standards that characterize Parmigiani's entire production.

PATEK PHILIPPE REF. 5079

This self-winding movement with Geneva Seal (Patek Philippe caliber R 27 PS) houses the minute repeater. The mechanical complexity of this watch led Patek Philippe to adopt the most refined and expensive technical solution: all the repeater mechanisms are housed by the pillar-plate itself and not by an additional module. Furthermore, the self-winding movement is equipped with a solid gold off-center rotor. Reference 5079, presented in 2001, has the case that had been created the year before to house the first chronograph-only watch of the Genevan master's recent history, characterized by a clean modern style and exceptional sizes. In fact, the 42mm diameter is quite unusual for Patek Philippe. The case size allows for the best possible results: the strokes of the Cathedral chime imitate perfectly the full and long lasting sounds of the bells of ancient cathedrals. Also attributing to this feat is the special alloy used for the acoustic gongs, characterized by high resonance values, developed by Patek Philippe and the metal experts of the Federal Swiss Institute of Technology of Lausanne.

Grand Complications

VACHERON CONSTANTIN REF. 30010

The minute repeater is one of Vacheron Constantin's specialties. This watch houses the manual-winding caliber 1755 and is produced in platinum or gold with drop-shaped lugs. Limited editions are common because only 2,090 repeater movements (also adopted for the perpetual-calendar repeater model) have been produced in cooperation with Dubois Dépraz.

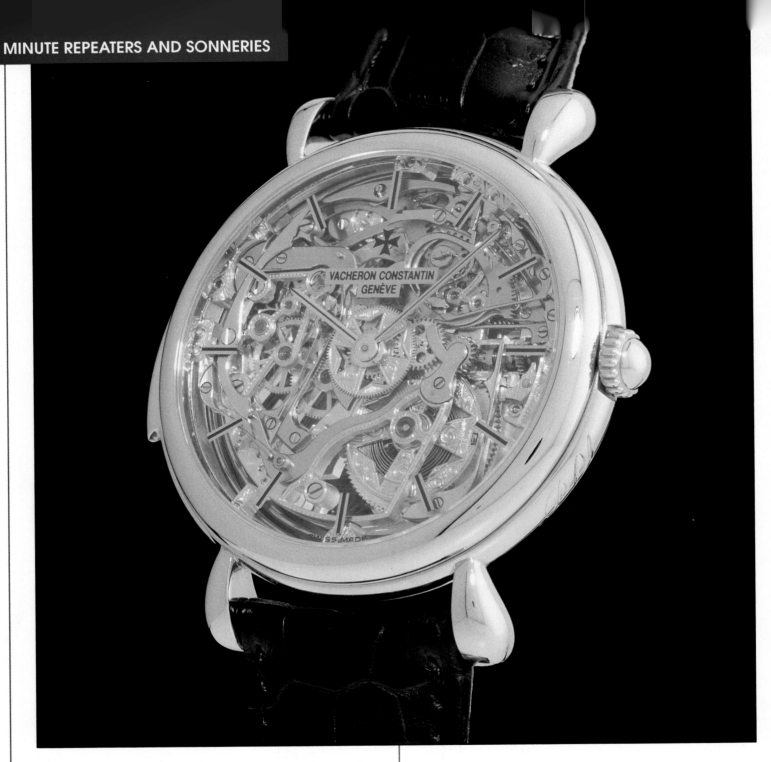

VACHERON CONSTANTIN REF. 30030

This minute repeater from the Historiques collection is a double masterwork of fine horology housing the caliber 1755 SQ. The sophisticated manual-winding movement provided with an hour, quarter and minute repeater is enriched by a refined skeleton finish and chasing of the bridges. The spectacular results are visible through both dial and caseback. The hour markers and the signature of the prestigious house are printed inside the protection glass.

VACHERON CONSTANTIN - TOUR DE L'ILE

Vacheron Constantin's master watchmakers invested more than 10,000 hours on research and development—almost two years—into this multi-complication. Only seven Tour de L'Ile watches will ever be created and each will house 834 individual parts and offer 16 complications that can be read off of a double-faced watch. The 47mm case houses the new Caliber 2750 with toubillon, minute repeater, moonphase, age of moon, perpetual calendar, second time zone, equation of time, sunrise, sunset, and sky chart. The watch was created in honor of the brand's 250th anniversary, celebrated in 2005.

VACHERON CONSTANTIN - MINUTE REPEATER PERPETUAL CALENDAR

REF. 1755QP

A proprietary Vacheron Constantin design, the minute-repeater caliber 13" features center hour and minute hands, two-position stem for winding and setting, and offers 40 hours of power reserve. Crafted in either 18-karat rose gold or platinum, the minute repeater features an open-worked decoration and strikes the hours, quarters and minutes on a pair of tiny hammers. The perpetual calendar offers hour, minute, date, day of week, month, moonphase, and takes into account leap years. The movement houses 30 jewels, and beats at a frequency of 18,000 vibrations per hour.

VACHERON CONSTANTIN - SKELETON MINUTE REPEATER REF. 1755SQ

Painstaking care has been lavished on every facet of this elaborate skeleton minute repeater. Both faces of the movement's mainplate are circular grained. Even the tiniest parts are hand polished and chamfered. With the touch of the slide, the watch discreetly chimes the hours, quarters and minutes. This watch is equipped with an all-or-nothing device so that when the slide bolt is activated, a toothed arm or rack is pushed. If it is not pushed all the way, no strike is heard, thereby assuring precision striking. The proprietary movement houses 30 jewels, offers 40 hours of power reserve and beats at 18,000 vibrations per hour.

EQUATIONS OF TIME

The equation-of-time function is extremely complex and offered very rarely. One of the most difficult complications to include in a wristwatch, the equation of time is based on sun time. Since the dawn of man, existence has related to the sun. However, since time is not consistent from one day to the next in relation to the meridian, an average day was fixed. The duration of an average day—also called an average sun day—was calculated based on the average of all the days in a year. Its duration of 24 hours does not vary.

The true sun day is the interval of time that passes between two consecutive passages of the sun at the meridian, which can vary from 14 minutes and 20 seconds to 16 minutes and 23 seconds.

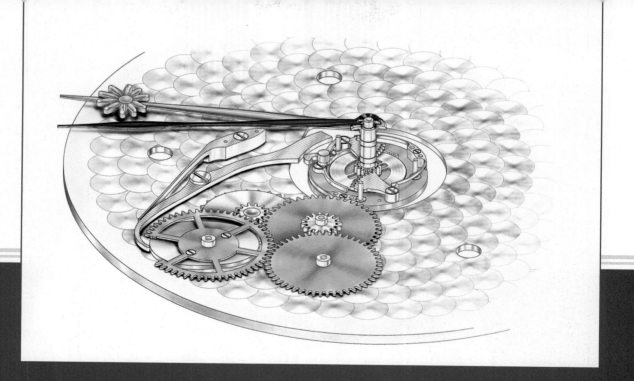

Extremely complex, the equation-of-time function indicates the difference between the average sun day and the true sun day for the wearer. This function has roots in astronomical clocks, but is a modern offering.

Only a handful of the finest watch companies offer equation of time in their timepieces due to the overwhelming nature of its tracking and readout. Those that do offer them, choose to present their readouts in a variety of manners.

AUDEMARS PIGUET - JULES AUDEMARS METROPOLIS QUANTIEME PERPETUEL

This extra-thin self-winding movement (A. P. 2130/2804 Caliber 2120/2808, base + equation and calendar modules) offers perpetual calendar (date, day, month, four-year cycle), world time, 24-hour indicator and day/night indicator. The basic movement of the Metropolis model is integrated by an innovative module combining a perpetual calendar with the world-time feature. On the silvered dial, the meridian and parallels are represented. The transparent caseback displays valuable decorations and a hand-chased skeleton rotor with a 21-karat gold sector. Water resistance is guaranteed up to 2atm.

AUDEMARS PIGUET - JULES AUDEMARS EQUATION OF TIME REF. 25934

This 18-karat gold Jules Audemars Equation of Time depicts mean solar time and real solar time, offers sunrise and sunset times (at 9:00 and 3:00 respectively), and perpetual calendar. It houses the self-winding caliber 2120/2808. Each subdial pointer is controlled by its own cam, and thus provides correct times only for the place which it has been adjusted. Each equation-of-time watch must be adjusted to correspond to the longitude and latitude of the location determined by its owner.

BREGUET - CLASSIQUE EQUATION OF TIME REF. 3477

This self-winding Breguet caliber 502DPE (Frédéric Piguet Cal. 71 base + patented QP module) offers equation of time, power reserve, and perpetual calendar (date, day in window, month, four-year cycle). In the upper part of the dial, two symmetric sectors display respectively the differences (expressed in minutes) between astronomic time and "conventional" time and the power reserve. At 9:00 the four-year cycle display is opposite to an oval zone at 3:00 with the individual watch number and the Breguet name. The impressive design also features center month and date at 6:00 and a digital display of the day of the week at 12:00. The indications displayed in characters may be read in English, French or German.

BLANCPAIN - EQUATION MARCHANTE

This Le Brassus Equation Marchante is the first wristwatch with running equation of time combined with an ultra-thin perpetual calendar and a retrograde moonphase display. The dial of the Le Brassus watch is fitted with two coaxial minute hands one that indicates mean solar time and another that indicates real solar time. The watch houses Blancpain's caliber 3863, which required several years in the development process and is comprised of nearly 400 parts, including 39 rubies. Equipped with 72 hours of power reserve, the watch is presented in a 42mm platinum case. The Equation Marchante is water resistant to 50 meters and created in a limited edition of 50 pieces.

DE BETHUNE - CS2

This 18-karat rose-gold timepiece is a masterful work of horological tradition. It houses a tourbillon, minute repeater, equation of time, and perpetual calendar. The tourbillon is visible through the sapphire caseback. The repeater function is fitted with a strike-silent mechanism and the gongs are tuned with each hammer. The equation of time is measured by the rose-gold center hand and is calculated with the latest astronomic indications. The 319-part manual-winding mechanism houses 20 jewels, a Swiss lever escapement, and Breguet spring balance. The mechanism is decorated with the Côtes de Genève pattern and offers 30 hours of power reserve. The silver dial is hand-guillochéd and features a rose-gold month display at 4:30 and date at 7:30.

JAEGER-LECOULTRE - GYROTOURBILLON I

Jaeger-LeCoultre's new patented GyroTourbillon I houses the complex 512-part Caliber 177 complete with a built-in running equation-of-time mechanism, as well as a host of other functions and indications. The exquisite escapement is a first in the of its kind in the history of the tourbillon with respect to its spherical design, whose multi-dimensional rotation is fascinating, as well as technical advancements. In addition to depicting the hours and minutes, the dial also indicates the remaining power reserve, date, month and true solar time as part of the equation-of-time function. The perpetual calendar won't require manual intervention until February 28, 2100. The spherical tourbillon features an aluminum case and an inner titanium and aluminum carriage that is positioned at a 90-degree angle to the outer case, and rotates 2.5 times faster than its companion. The total weight of this spherical wonder is just 0.33 grams.

JAQUET DROZ - EQUATION OF TIME

This Equation of Time depicts the true complexity of time. No day is comprised of exactly the same amount of seconds and minutes. Rather than simply depict the calendar in 24-hour days, the equation-of-time function accounts for the real solar time changes and depicts the real solar time along with the mean solar time. With Jaquet Droz's Equation of Time, the difference between real and mean solar times is illustrated cleanly and uniquely.

VACHERON CONSTANTIN - TOUR DE L'ILE

Vacheron Constantin's master watchmakers invested more than 10,000 hours on research and development—almost two years into this multi-complication. Only seven Tour de L'Ile watches will ever be created and each will house 834 individual parts and offer 16 complications that can be read off of a double-faced watch. The 47mm case houses the new Caliber 2750 with toubillon, minute repeater, moonphase, age of moon, perpetual calendar, second time zone, equation of time, sunrise, sunset, and sky chart. The watch was created in honor of the brand's 250th anniversary, celebrated in 2005.

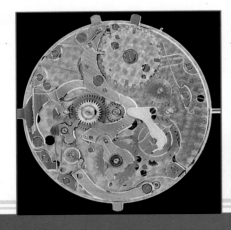

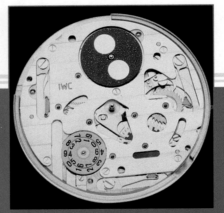

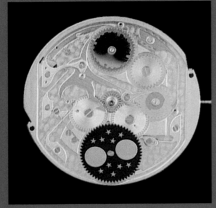

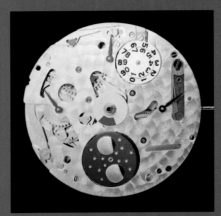

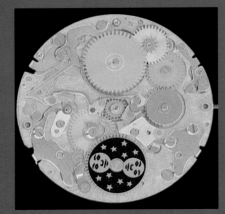

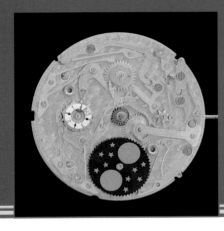

As the world progresses, simply tracking hours, minutes and seconds is not enough. It also is important to be able to track days, dates, years and leap years. Hence, the perpetual calendar wristwatch.

PERPETUAL CALENDARS

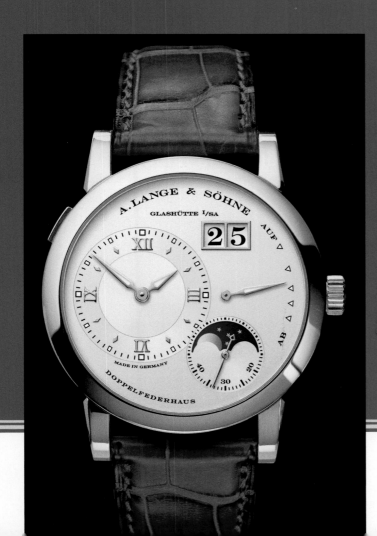

Invaluable in today's fast-paced world, the perpetual calendar watch has gained incredible popularity. Essentially, the perpetual calendar automatically tracks and displays the day, month, and date. Most perpetual calendar watches also track the moon's phases and self-adjusting for short months and leap years.

Calendar systems in timepieces date back to the early 15th century, when astronomical clock towers inspired clock makers to incorporate additional time-tracking functions into their masterpieces. Throughout the centuries, a host of different calendars have been developed and translated into timepieces. Watchmakers of the 1700s and early 1800s wrestled with obstacles inherent in calendar watches, such as how to advance the date automatically or how to accommodate leap years. In fact, prior to the advent of the perpetual calendar, most calendar watches required some sort of manual adjustment at the end of the month because of their varying lengths.

While Breguet registered his self-winding perpetual watch with calendar in the year 1795, the development of the perpetual calendar system is generally credited to Louis Audemars in1853 (though Audemars's development was not realized until 1860). The original system devised by Audemars (and since perfected by several companies) features a circular cam consisting of 48 months accounting for differences in dates.

Most perpetual calendar watches today consist of a date wheel, date-change lever, a day wheel, day-of-the-week lever and an intermediate month wheel with month rack disc and finger.

Complicated perpetual calendar watches can track time for centuries without needing adjustments. Predominantly, perpetual calendar watches of today are built to track time until the year 2100, when manual adjustments will have to be made (ideally on March 1) because of changes introduced with the Gregorian calendar, which ensure that real time and solar time will coincide correctly. Simply put, the year 2100 would normally be scheduled to fall as a leap year—but 2100 is not divisible by four, the requirement imposed by the Gregorian calendar for leap years. With a few spectacular exceptions, manual adjustments will have to be made to perpetual calendars to compensate for this break in the 4-year cycle and the loss of February 29, 2100.

The impulse causes the date wheel to advance within its 31 teeth by one position. At the same time, the day-of-the-week lever pushes the day wheel, and so on.

Most perpetual calendar watches today consist of a date wheel, date-change lever, a day wheel, day-of-the-week lever and an intermediate month wheel with month rack disc and finger. There are also year and decade discs and a moonphase indicator in some perpetual calendar watches. The micro technology of perpetual calendars is incredibly complicated—with the entire disc-and-lever system linked together. Simplified, each night a switching impulse is transmitted from the main movement of the watch via a tiny lever, pulling on the date-change lever. The impulse causes the date wheel to advance within its 31 teeth by one position. At the same time, the day-of-the-week lever pushes the day wheel, and so on.

Certain complications arise in the making of perpetual calendar watches with regard to setting the functions and read-

outs if the watch winds down. Typically, watchmakers handle these problems differently and perpetual calendar watches are often different in their ultimate composition.

Several watchmakers, including Jaeger-LeCoultre, Patek Philippe and Ulysse Nardin have successfully dealt with the issue of overcoming an open adjustment in the year 2100. Jaeger-LeCoultre's Master Perpetual watch houses an automatic movement with a pushpiece mechanism that enables the wearer to reprogram the entire calendar. In addition to the other functions, this watch also offers decade readout.

Companies such as Breguet and IWC also offer year-readouts on their perpetual calendars, and IWC even has a century slide indicator on its 500-year Da Vinci watch—although it's doubtful any one user will live to see it change more than once. Offering a whole new technology, Breguet unveiled the patented In-Line Perpetual Calendar wristwatch with instant year change. The new movement aligns the year indication on the dial to the corresponding position of the functions on the calendar plate, thus allowing the year hand to jump instantly from one year to the next without legibility problems.

Patek Philippe has developed a secular perpetual calendar that runs on the full 400-year cycle of the Gregorian calendar and never needs resetting. A wheel in the movement makes just one revolution every four centuries.

Blancpain's perpetual calendar requires a minor one-day correction just once early in the year 2100, representing a perpetual calendar efficient for more than 200 years. The perpetual calendar's mechanical memory operates via a small satellite wheel that makes one revolution every four years.

IWC has developed an all-new way to present the moonphases of both hemispheres in its Portuguese Perpetual Calendar, Ref. 5021. This watch combines the company's 5000 caliber movement, which obtains its energy from the renowned Pellaton winding mechanism, with the perpetual calendar in a

Patek Philippe has developed a secular perpetual calendar that runs on the full 400-year cycle of the Gregorian calendar and never needs resetting. A wheel in the movement makes just one revolution every four centuries.

patented world-first that was unveiled in 2003.

IWC's Schaffhausen watch-makers developed an entirely new representation of the moonphase for this oversized perpetual calendar watch. Previously, moonphase displays appeared in a single aperture—depicting a crescent-shaped moon in the dial that rotates to depict the heavenly body as seen in the sky of the Northern Hemisphere. IWC's invention shows the position of the moon in both hemispheres. The system is made possible by a design feature that is still unique to IWC: a multi-tiered disc with two opposing circular windows, rotating above a yellow surface with two identical black circular areas lying in the horizontal plane representing the moon. The result is two moonphase displays on the watch dial that are constantly in motion. The top aperture depicts the moon's phases in the Northern Hemisphere, and the lower aperture offers a true-to-side representation of the moon's phases in the Southern Hemisphere.

Some complicated perpetual calendars also include astronomical indicators and others include equations of time. Most include moonphase readouts, and some calendar watches feature only moonphase readouts (included in this chapter).

Perhaps the most self-explanatory of all complications, the moonphase display shows just that. It operates via a small disc within the case that bears the phases of the moon. As the disc rotates it reveals the proper moonphase for the progressing month. The wearer views the phases of the moon via a window aperture on the dial. Some watchmakers hand enamel their moonphase discs, while others create them of semi-precious stones such as lapis lazuli.

A. LANGE & SÖHNE - CABARET MOONPHASE

An impressive scenic rendering of the waxing and waning moon appears on the Cabaret watch. The rectangular timepiece already offers outsized date via a patented twin-disc mechanism hidden beneath the double aperture at 12:00. The added moonphase display is positioned at 6:00. The Cabaret Moonphase houses the caliber L931.5 movement, which is decorated almost entirely by hand. It is composed of 268 parts, 31 jewels and a lever escapement. It offers 42 hours of power reserve.

A. LANGE & SÖHNE - LANGE 1 MOONPHASE

The Lange 1 Moonphase features a display that is continuously driven by the hour wheel. Its deviation from the moon's true orbit is only one day per 122.6 years. It is one of the most accurate moonphase watches ever built.

A. LANGE & SÖHNE - LANGEMATIK PERPETUAL

The Langematik Perpetual is the first and only wristwatch that combines a perpetual calendar with the Lange outsized date, the zero-reset time-setting mechanism, and a main pushpiece that advances all calendar indications in one-day intervals. The self-winding caliber L922.1 movement, also known as the Sax-O-Mat, is comprised of 478 components. The moonphase display deviates only one day in 122 years.

A. LANGE & SÖHNE - LANGEMATIK PERPETUAL

This self-winding A. Lange & Söhne caliber L922.1 features oversized date, day, month, and offers four-year cycle and moonphase indicators. The Sax-O-Mat movement, combined with a calendar module (Lange's own production), is covered by two patents: one for the oversized date and another for its zero-reset system. The different indications can be corrected two ways: individually by actuating the relevant correctors and simultaneously by the pusher at 10:00, which advances them all in one-day increments.

AUDEMARS PIGUET - ROYAL OAK PERPETUAL CALENDAR REF. 25820ST

This self-winding Royal Oak Perpetual Calendar watch houses the extra-thin caliber 2120/2802 movement with an 18-karat white-gold skeleton rotor. The steel-cased watch offers date, day, month, year, leap year and moonphase display. Water resistant to 20 meters, the watch features a gray dial and steel bracelet.

AUDEMARS PIGUET - JULES AUDEMARS GRANDE COMPLICATION
REF. 258660R

The elegant Jules Audemars Grande Complication is powered by the self-winding Caliber 2885 with more than 600 components. The watch offers perpetual calendar, minute repeater, and split-second chronograph. It is housed in 18-karat pink gold and features five correctors and a slide for the repeater on the side. The month and four-year cycle are at 6:00 and the moonphase and date are at 12:00. This watch is also available in platinum.

AUDEMARS PIGUET - JULES AUDEMARS METROPOLIS QUANTIEME PERPETUEL

This extra-thin self-windng movement (A. P. 2130/2804 Caliber 2120/2808, base + equation and calendar modules) offers perpetual calendar (date, day, month, four-year cycle), world time, 24-hour indicator and day/night indicator. The basic movement of the Metropolis model is integrated by an innovative module combining a perpetual calendar with the world-time feature. On the silvered dial, the meridian and parallels are represented. The transparent caseback displays valuable decorations and a hand-chased skeleton rotor with a 21-karat gold sector. Water resistance is guaranteed up to 2atm.

AUDEMARS PIGUET - ROYAL OAK SKELETON PERPETUAL CALENDAR

REF. 25829

This Royal Oak model displays the date, day, month, moonphases and leap years. Its open-worked movement Caliber 2120/2802 features a 21-karat gold rotor segment and engraved rotor. The case and bracelet are stainless steel, the case's assembly screws in 18-karat gold. Water resistant to 20 meters, the Royal Oak Skeleton Perpetual Calendar features a sapphire crystal and caseback and its transparent sapphire dial reveals the engraved work of the movement.

BLANCPAIN - EQUATION MARCHANTE

This Le Brassus Equation Marchante is the first wristwatch with running equation of time combined with an ultra-thin perpetual calendar and a retrograde moonphase display. The dial of the Le Brassus watch is fitted with two coaxial minute hands—one that indicates mean solar time and another that indicates real solar time. The watch houses Blancpain's caliber 3863, which required several years in the development process and is comprised of nearly 400 parts, including 39 rubies. Equipped with 72 hours of power reserve, the watch is presented in a 42mm platinum case. The Equation Marchante is water resistant to 50 meters and created in a limited edition of 50 pieces.

BLANCPAIN - LE BRASSUS PERPETUAL CALENDAR CHRONOGRAPH

This self-winding Blancpain caliber 56P9U (1185 base + 56QP module) offers perpetual calendar (date, day, month, four-year cycle and moonphase readout), and flyback split-second chronograph. This limited-edition model has a platinum case and closed back in an extra-large size (42mm). On the opaline dial, calendar and chronograph information appears in an analog big-size display assuring the best possible readability. The chronograph is provided with an additional split-second hand.

BLANCPAIN - VILLERET QUANTIÈME PERPETUEL

This poprietary self-winding Frédéric Piguet caliber 5453 offers date, day, four-year leap cycle and moonphase readout. This simple and elegant collection is characterized by a round case with rounded steps and curl-shaped lugs—a discrete whole that has been housing all of the Blancpain watches for many years since the beginnings of their revival (by Piguet) in the 1980s. The small workshop in the Vallée de Joux wanted to produce a series of watches featuring each of the six specialties of horology, among which is the perpetual calendar with moonphase indications.

BLANCPAIN - VILLERET ANNIVERSAIRE 1601

This proprietary self-winding Frédéric Piguet caliber 5453 offers date, day, four-year leap cycle and moonphase readout. The basic movement of this perpetual-calendar watch with 100 hours of autonomy is provided with a calendar module slightly modified with respect to the one traditionally adopted, in order to realize the function of the leap-year cycle in a window. The model has the same excellent legibility as its peers from the first generation. The date and day of the week, i.e. the indications most frequently read, are suitably sized and positioned on both dial sides.

BREGUET - CLASSIQUE PERPETUAL CALENDAR REF. 5327

The Classique Perpetual Calendar houses an improved self-winding movement with 46 hours of power reserve, and stunning moonphase readout. Cased in 18-karat yellow gold, the watch features a sapphire caseback and is water resistant to 30 meters. The dial is engine-turned silvered 18-karat gold and features a secret-signature chapter ring with Roman hours. The date, day and leap years are indicated via three subdials, while there is a central month indicator. The power-reserve indicator is at 10:30. The watch is powered by the ultra-thin automatic, 12-ligne, 38-jeweled caliber 502.3DRP1. It is hand engraved and numbered. The gold rotor is hand engraved and there is a straight-line lever escapement. The timepiece is also available in 18-karat white gold.

BREGUET - CLASSIQUE QUANTIEME PERPETUAL IN-LINE

This self-winding movement (Breguet caliber 502QPL, Frédéric Piguet caliber 71 base + Breguet calendar module) features date, day, four-year leap cycle and moonphase readout. This patented movement, provided with a guilloché off-center rotor, features all the calendar indications on the same straight line for the first time in the history of horology. On the vertical dial axis the following displays are arranged from top to bottom: the day of the week in a window, the subdials for month and date. The latter encloses the turning disc for the four-year cycle indication.

BREGUET - CLASSIQUE QUANTIEME PERPERPETUAL RETROGRADE

This self-winding movement (Breguet caliber 591QPT, Lemania caliber 8826 base + Breguet calendar module) is equipped with date, day, four-year leap cycle and moonphase readout. Its analog date is indicated by a retrograde serpentine hand, while the day and month indications are digital as the four-year cycle, whose window is placed in a unusual position between 1:00 and 2:00. Each leap year is indicated by a red pointer.

CARTIER - TORTUE PERPETUAL CALENDAR

Among the newest complex watches from Cartier is the stunning extra-wide Tortue Perpetual Calendar. Crafted in pure platinum or in 18-karat rose gold, the Tortue Perpetual Calendar with Two Time Zones houses the 9421MC mechanical movement. The intricate double-complication movement is comprised of 276 parts and 27 jewels. Complete with 18-karat gold rotor, the watch is equipped with 49 hours of power reserve, features an 18-karat gold dial with Roman numerals, a faceted sapphire crown and a sapphire caseback. The movement and case of each timepiece consist of matching numbers.

CHOPARD - PERPETUAL CALENDAR WITH SEASONS

This self-winding movement (caliber 889/2152, Jaeger-LeCoultre 889/2 base + chronograph and calendar modules developed by Chopard and Dubois Dépraz) also offers perpetual calendar (date, day, month, week, season, four-year cycle, moonphase), and chronograph with three counters. This limited edition watch is characterized by a big-size case with two curved lugs, rectangular pushers and sapphire crystal caseback. The rotor is equipped with a 21-karat yellow-gold sector, skeletonized, decorated with a circular-graining pattern and personalized "Chopard."

DE BETHUNE - SPLIT-SECONDS CHRONOGRAPH, PERPETUAL CALENDAR CS1

This split-seconds chronograph, minute-counter, and perpetual calendar with large date is a complicated watch offering exceptional legibility. It is the first watch in the De Bethune line to be fitted with a perpetual calendar and large date function. Crafted in 18-karat rose gold, the watch is 42mm in diameter and features an octagonal crown with included pusher for the split-seconds function. The 294-part movement features a Swiss lever escapement and 27 jewels, offers 30 hours of power reserve and is decorated with the Côtes de Genève pattern. The watch features hours and minutes, split-seconds chronograph, 30-minute counter at 3:00, month at 6:00, subseconds at 9:00, and date at 12:00. Winding and time setting are adjusted by the crown in two positions.

DE BETHUNE - CS2

This 18-karat rose-gold timepiece is a masterful work of horological tradition. It houses a tourbillon, minute repeater, equation of time, and perpetual calendar. The tourbillon is visible through the sapphire caseback. The repeater function is fitted with a strike-silent mechanism and the gongs are tuned with each hammer. The equation of time is measured by the rose-gold center hand and is calculated with the latest astronomic indications. The 319-part manual-winding mechanism houses 20 jewels, a Swiss lever escapement, and Breguet spring balance. The mechanism is decorated with the Côtes de Genève pattern and offers 30 hours of power reserve. The silver dial is hand-guilloché and features a rose-gold month display at 4:30 and date at 7:30.

DE BETHUNE - PERPETUAL CALENDAR WITH REVOLVING MOON PHASE DB 15

Housed in a 43mm, 18-karat white-gold case, this perpetual calendar demonstrates unique solutions in watch-making. A most interesting aspect is the original moonphase design: a sphere (globe) made of platinum and steel, revolving on its own axis in a dial with leap-year indication. The perpetual calendar movement is manufactured entirely in De Bethune's atelier, and is fitted with an additional function that allows quick setting of the date through the crown in the third position. The leap-year function is depicted by the color change of the star under the moon, depending on the year. The mechanism was developed in-house, and constitutes the Caliber 30 with double barrel—the thinnest in the world—and has a unique balance spring and regulation. The manual-winding movement features a new Swiss lever escapement, beats at 28,800 vibrations per hour, offers four days of power reserve, and houses 24 jewels. Winding and time-setting functions are adjusted via the crown in three positions.

Perpetual Calendars

FRANCK MULLER - 1200 QP LONG ISLAND

This self-winding movement (Franck Muller caliber 2800 base + Dubois Dépraz module) offers day, date, four-year leap cycle and moonphase readout. The indications of this traditional perpetual-calendar watch are displayed inside the rectangle of the Long Island collection, a family in which the most classical complication was recently introduced. The automatic movement is equipped with a platinum rotor. The 43mm model is offered in platinum and four colors of gold.

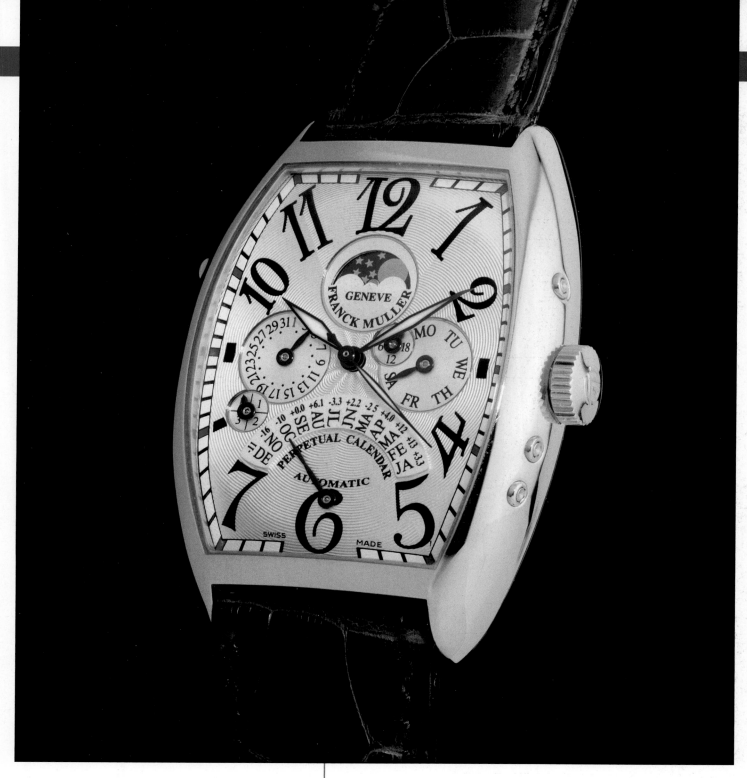

FRANCK MULLER - CC7851 QP E

This self-winding movement (Franck Muller caliber 7000 base + exclusive Dubois Dépraz calendar module) features date, day, retrograde month, four-year cycle and moonphase. Within the Cintrée Curvex family, this perpetual-calendar model is supplied with a retrograde months hand and an additional 24-hour subdial. The indications displayed above the months scale refer to the equation of time, i.e. they indicate the maximum (+ or -) differences, between civil and solar time, expressed in minutes, during the specific month indicated.

FRANCK MULLER - CC75850 QP 24

This self-winding movement (Franck Muller caliber 2800 base + exclusive Dubois Dépraz 5100 calendar module) offers date, day, four-year leap cycle and moonphase readout. Luminescent numerals characterize this Casablanca version (shown here), while they are printed in black in the standard version. The automatic movement, provided with a platinum oscillating mass, gives the usual calendar information, integrated by the 24-hour feature shown on an additional subdial.

FRANCK MULLER - CINTRÉE CURVEX CHRONOGRAPH BI-RETROGRADE PERPETUAL CALENDAR

This self-winding movement (FM 5888 BR, Franck Muller 7000 base + Dubois Dépraz exclusive calendar module) offers perpetual calendar (retrograde date and day, month, four-year cycle, moonphase) and chronograph with three counters. It is equipped with an automatic movement with 950 platinum rotor and a chronograph time display up to 12 hours and 30 minutes. The guilloché dial, covered by a translucent enamel layer, with silvered subdials and mother-of-pearl inlays, displays the original retrograde indications of the day of the week and date. Leap year is indicated digitally and shares its position at 12:00 with the month hand.

FRANCK MULLER - CINTRÉE CURVEX CHRONOGRAPH PERPETUAL CALENDAR

This self-winding movement (Franck Muller caliber 7000 + Dubois Dépraz calendar module) offers perpetual calendar (date, day, retrograde month, four-year cycle, moonphase) and chronograph with one counter. The model was first created in 1999 and is characterized by the basic movement (a self-winding chronograph with a platinum rotor) as well as the exclusive patented perpetual-calendar module, with a retrograde month hand and 24-hour subdial. The original dial setting features a circular sexagesimal scale in two colors and showing divisions for 1/5 of a second. The caseback is guilloché and the ring with the typical Arabic numerals is brushed.

F.P. JOURNE - OCTA ANNUAL CALENDAR

As with all masterpieces from F.P Journe, the Octa Annual Calendar reveals watchmaker François-Paul Journe's unique creativity both in dial design and the movement's subtlety. The automatic F.P. Journe 1300 caliber with 5-day power reserve displays the date, which requires one adjustment at the end of February. Time indications are displayed on the dial's right side, the calendar is marked by two windows for day and month on the left, the flyback date hand is centered.

GÉRALD GENTA - ARENA SPORT GMT PERPETUAL CALENDAR

This Arena Sport GMT Perpetual Calendar has a 45mm titanium case with platinum bezel. It is equipped with an automatic movement with perpetual calendar. A 24-hour dial at 12:00 serves as a second time-zone indicator. It offers 45 hours of power reserve.

GÉRALD GENTA - ARENA SPORT TOURBILLON PERPETUAL CALENDAR MOONPHASE

From the Arena Sport collection, this Tourbillon Perpetual Calendar watch hosts scintillating subdials and chapter rings on its dial. Crafted in platinum with a palladium bezel, the watch is equipped with a proprietary tourbillon automatic movement developed internally. It features a perpetual calendar. The dial offers indications for moonphase, leap years and months, days of the month, days of the week and small seconds. The movement is coated in antique gold and decorated with a concentric circular graining. The watch has 64 hours of power reserve and is water resistant to 10atm.

GIRARD-PERREGAUX - G.P. POUR FERRARI "F310B" CHRONOGRAPH

PERPETUAL CALENDAR

This self-winding Girard-Perregaux caliber 3170 (3100 base + calendar and chronograph modules) offers perpetual calendar (date, day, month on four-year cycle, moonphase), chronograph with three counters and tachometer scale. The affinities existing between Girard-Perregaux and Ferrari are brought to life in the titanium model dedicated to the F1 "F310B" and bear witness to the brands' shared will to overcome and control technology, materials and shapes in their respective extreme expressions. The dial is carbon fiber, an advanced material often used in the aeronautic and automotive industries, particularly for race cars.

GIRARD-PERREGAUX - OPERA TWO REF. 99740

The Opera Two features a perpetual calendar in addition to the Opera One's carillon Westminster, minute repeater, and Tourbillon with three gold Bridges. The Opera Two is encased in platinum or pink, yellow, or white gold. Three of the four strike hammers are always visible through the dial and the fourth hammer can be seen when the striking mechanism is operated. The extraordinary complexity of the refined tourbillon movement can be admired through the watch's sapphire caseback. The perpetual calendar indicates the hours and minutes, the day of the week, dates and months, as well as the leap-year cycle. The GP9897 caliber offers 80 hours of power reserve and beats at 21,600 vibrations per hour.

GIRARD-PERREGAUX - RICHEVILLE PERPETUAL CALENDAR REF. 27220

The 18-karat gold tonneau-shaped Richeville case houses the perpetual calendar automatic GP033Q0 movement with 27 jewels and 50 hours of power reserve, which beats at 28,800 vibrations per hour with incredible accuracy. The watch displays moonphase at 6:00 and is water resistant to 30 meters.

GIRARD-PERREGAUX - TRIBUTE TO ENZO FERRARI TOURBILLON WITH PERPETUAL CALENDAR REF. 99190

The Tribute to Enzo Ferrari Tourbillon with three gold Bridges is created in honor of the new Enzo Ferrari automobile and marks a 10-year alliance between the companies. The Enzo Ferrari Tourbillon is enhanced with a variety of functions, including a chronograph and a perpetual calendar. The watch houses the GP9982 manual-winding movement and offers 70 hours of power reserve. The barrel is decorated with a motif replicating the Enzo's engine. The watch is available in either platinum or 18-karat gold, both with a carbon fiber dial and calendar readout using the same color scheme as the Enzo Ferrari instrument panel. The 43mm case is water resistant to 30 meters.

Perpetual Calendars

GIRARD-PERREGAUX - VINTAGE 1945 KING SIZE PERPETUAL CALENDAR

REF. 90285

The Vintage 1945 King Size with Perpetual Calendar is water resistant to 30 meters and houses the 27-jeweled GP 33Q0.D movement beating at 28,800 vibrations per hour. The 18-karat white-gold timepiece has a power reserve of 50 hours.

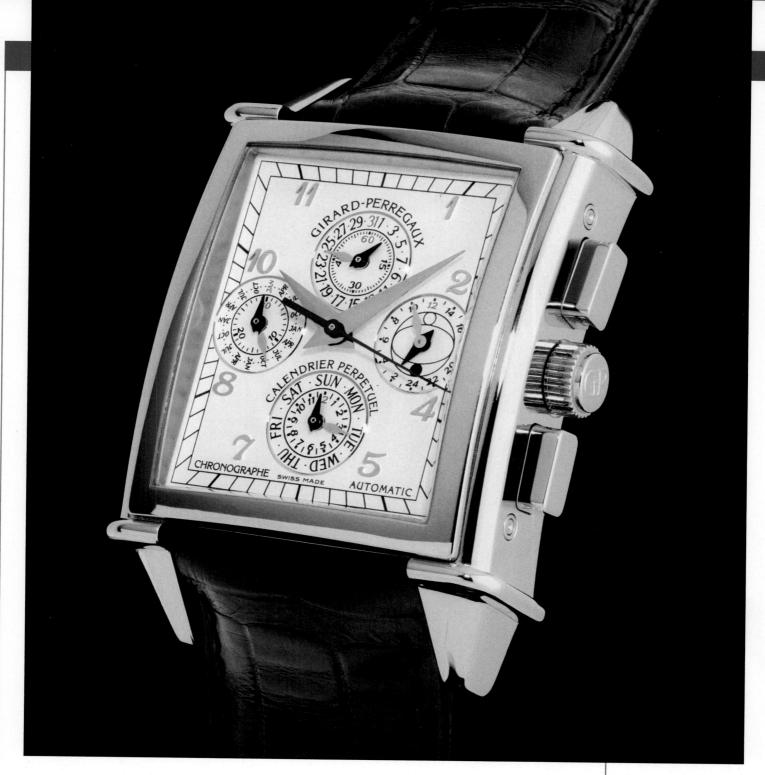

GIRARD-PERREGAUX - VINTAGE 1945 XXL PERPETUAL CALENDAR CHRONOGRAPH 90270

Girard Perregaux launched XXL size in 2003 to housing a couple of extrahordinary complicated movements. The Tourbillon Magistral and this Perpetual Calendar Chronograph. A full analogic display with the four subdials showing two information each, all powered by the GP 3170 caliber.

GIRARD-PERREGAUX - VINTAGE 1945 XXL TOURBILLON

PERPETUAL CALENDAR REF. 99860

Housed in the extra large 18-karat gold Vintage 1945 case, this manual-winding GP9800 caliber watch features a tourbillon and perpetual calendar. The date readout is at 3:00, moonphase at 6:00, days of the week at 9:00, and month at 12:00. The watch offers 70 hours of power reserve and is water resistant to 30 meters.

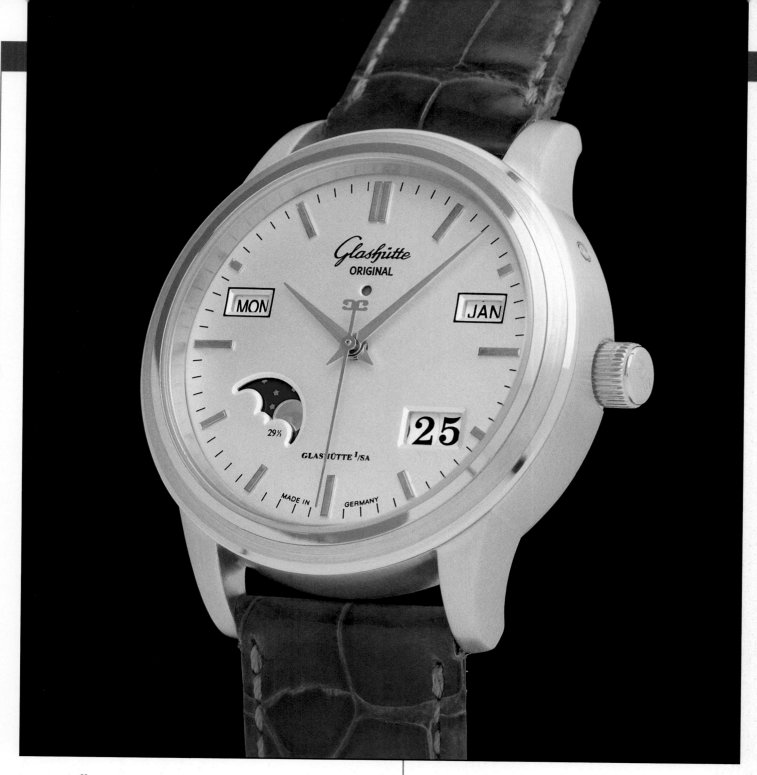

GLASHÜTTE ORIGINAL - SENATOR KLASSIK

This self-winding Glashütte Original caliber 39-50 offers oversized date, day, month, four-year leap cycle and moonphase readout. The caliber, with an autonomy of 40 hours and provided with a rotor whose sector is 21-karat gold, is used only as a basic movement for complicated watches. A primary characteristic of the Saxon manufacture, in addition to the famous "Glashütte polish," is the main bridge known as a three-quarter pillar-plate (because it covers three quarters of the total surface). The entire movement has a diameter of 30.95mm—while the basic is only 26mm—and a thickness of 7.2mm (compared to the 4.3mm-thick basic movement). An original element is the arrangement of the indications: day and month in lateral windows, red leap-year indicator placed above the hands' pivot, date display with two coaxial and complanar discs at 4:00, opposite the moonphase at 8:00.

Perpetual Calendars

HARRY WINSTON - PREMIER PERPETUAL CALENDAR TIMEZONE

Perpetuating the tradition of the Premier collection, Harry Winston combines the perpetual calendar function with two time zones in this model. The perpetual calendar indicates the date and day on small dials at 3:00 and 9:00 respectively, while the months and leap years are displayed at 12:00. The second time zone appears at 6:00 on a dual-colored day/night 24-hour counter. The GMT function is set using a screw-on pushpiece. The perpetual calendar will function without adjustment until February 28, 2100. The watch, with automatic GP3306 movement, is crafted in an edition of 55 18-karat white-gold pieces and 45 18-karat rose-gold pieces.

HARRY WINSTON OPUS 4

The fourth in Harry Winston's ingenious Opus series of timepieces developed in conjunction with independent watchmakers, the Opus 4 is a true grand complication. Created with Christophe Claret, the master of chiming watches, the Opus 4 is a completely reversible minute-repeater striking on cathedral gongs. One face of the watch reveals the tourbillon and the other features a large moonphase indication with date. The movement, which reverses the direction of the hands for each face, is housed in a platinum Premier case signed by Harry Winston. It is comprised of 423 parts, including 40 jewels, and has 53 hours of power reserve. The Ø 44mm case is water resistant to 30 meters and features a mechanism that allows its reversal. Only 18 platinum Opus 4 models and two high-jeweled versions will be created.

Perpetual Calendars

IWC - GRANDE COMPLICATION 3770

This grand complication watch offers chronograph, perpetual calendar, perpetual moonphase indicator, four-digit year indicator, minute repeater and small second with stop device. It houses the caliber 79091 movement with 75 jewels and 44 hours of power reserve. The watch beats at 28,800 vibrations per hour.

ALTERNATE VERSION: 9270 IN PLATINUM WITH PLATINUM BRACELET.

IWC - GST PERPETUAL CALENDAR

This self-winding IWC caliber 79261 (Valjoux 7750 base + IWC calendar module) is equipped with perpetual calendar (date, day, month, four-digit year, moonphase) and chronograph with three counters. It is a high-tech multi-complicated watch. This perpetual-calendar chronograph is available in titanium with a black dial or in stainless steel with a salmon or gray rhodium-plated dial. It is water resistant up to 12atm and its movement is shockproof and antimagnetic according to the standards (NICHS 91-101) in force in the watchmaking sector.

IWC PORTUGUESE PERPETUAL CALENDAR

This Portuguese Perpetual Calendar watch house the brand's 5000 caliber and offers ingenious displays. It houses the Pellaton winding mechanism with an entirely new moonphase display—a world-first patent obtained by IWC for this 2003 launch. The perpetual calendar watch offers seven days of power reserve and offers all perpetual calendar readouts. The moonphase is represented in the sky's Northern Hemisphere and in the Southern Hemisphere as well via a disc display with two opposing circular windows rotating above a yellow surface with two black circles. Both moons are constantly in motion. The watch is offered in all three colors of gold.

IWC - GST PERPETUAL CALENDAR REF. 3756

This GST Perpetual Calendar watch houses the 79261 movement with 39 jewels, offering 44 hours of power reserve. Its automatic movement is equipped with perpetual calendar, perpetual moonphase display, four-digit year display, mechanical chronograph and pushbutton-release safety clasp. It is crafted in titanium with a sapphire case.

IWC - DA VINCI REF. 3758

This Da Vinci offers perpetual moonphase indication, four-year digit indication, chronograph, small second with stop device. It houses the caliber 79261 with 39 jewels and 44 hours of power reserve. The automatic movement oscillates at 28,800 vibrations per hour. This watch is water resistant to 30 meters and is crafted in steel or gold.

JAEGER-LECOULTRE - GYROTOURBILLON I

Jaeger-LeCoultre's new patented GyroTourbillon I houses the Caliber 177 complete with a built-in running equation-of-time mechanism, as well as a host of other functions and indications. The exquisite escapement is a first in the history of the tourbillon due to its spherical design, whose multi-dimensional rotation is fascinating, as well as technically advanced. The complex caliber is comprised of 512 parts. In addition to depicting the hours and minutes, its dial also indicates the remaining power reserve, date, month and true solar time as part of the equation-of-time function. The perpetual calendar won't require manual intervention until February 28, 2100. The spherical tourbillon features an aluminum case and an inner titanium and aluminum carriage that is oriented at a 90-degree angle to the outer case, and rotates 2.5 times faster than its companion. The total weight of the nearly 100 components that comprise this spherical wonder is just 0.33 grams.

Perpetual Calendars

JAEGER-LECOULTRE - MASTER GRAND MEMOVOX

This self-winding movement (Jaeger-LeCoultre Caliber 9091, 918 base + 44 calendar module) offers perpetual calendar (date, day, month, two-digit year, moonphase), and alarm. The movement of this highly complicated watch is based on the combination of the Caliber 918, the only alarm system provided with a dedicated gong, with a perpetual-calendar module. It consists of 349 components and, as are all Master models, is tested for 1,000 hours. The crown at 4:00 winds the watch, the one at 2:00 (counterclockwise) winds the alarm system and sets the hand, while a corrector at 8:00 advances all of the calendar data forward by one day at the same time. The hand at 6:00 is used to indicate the 24 hours and shows the time section (marked in red) suitable for calendar corrections.

JAEGER-LECOULTRE - MASTER PERPETUAL

The Master Perpetual's self-winding Jaeger-LeCoultre Caliber 889/440/2 offers date, month, two-digit year, day and moonphase. The manufacture movement, tested over 1,000 hours, displays the year by two digits and features a center consent indicator in a window: when the sector is red, the hours indicated are unsuitable for calendar adjustments by the corrector placed at 8:00. An aperture at the base of the main hands allows reading inside the window.

Perpetual Calendars

JAEGER-LECOULTRE - MASTER EIGHT DAYS PERPETUAL

Classically designed, this Master Eight Days Perpetual watch houses the mechanical manually wound Caliber 876 that is crafted, assembled and decorated by hand. It beats at 28,800 vibrations per hour and consists of 262 parts and 37 jewels. It offers hours, minutes, date, month, day of week, four-digit year display, moonphase, power reserve, and a day/night indicator with red safety zone for changing of the perpetual calendar. The watch is crafted in platinum or in 18-karat pink gold.

JAEGER-LECOULTRE - REVERSO QP

This manual-winding Jaeger-LeCoultre Caliber 855 offers retrograde date, day, month, four-year cycle, moonphase and day/night indicator. The movement of the Reverso Quantième, entirely designed and constructed by Jaeger-LeCoultre and consisting of 276 elements, is designed specifically for the rectangular case. Its components are assembled by layers, taking advantage of the two dials: one for the hour, day-night and leap-year indications and the other for the day-month, retrograde date and moonphase display. Both are provided with fast correctors.

JAQUET DROZ - LES LUNES EMAIL

This unusual Jaquet Droz watch features a calendar with days and months through an aperture and a pointer-type date. It also features an interesting moonphase readout via a retrograde hand and circular moon-depiction apertures. The watch houses the Jaquet Droz caliber 6553-4 self-winding mechanical movement with 28 jewels and beating at 28,800 vibrations per hour. The 40.5mm, 18-karat white-gold watch offers 72 hours of power reserve. Each piece is numbered individually and water resistant to 100 feet.

PARMIGIANI FLEURIER - TECNICA XIV RED FLAMINGO

This unique piece is a manual-winding, 38-jeweled tourbillon that features a minute repeater on two gongs. Beating at 21,600 vibrations per hour, the PF351.02 movement offers 45 hours of power reserve. It also offers perpetual calendar in addition to hour and minute readouts. The 42mm case is crafted in 950 platinum and is double fluted. Water resistant to 30 meters, it features a sapphire crystal and caseback and is entirely hand engraved and decorated. The Tecnica XIV Red Flamingo's caseback is covered with translucent red enamel and numbered individually. The hand-engraved dial is 18-karat gold.

PARMIGIANI FLEURIER - TORIC RETROGRADE PERPETUAL CALENDAR

This perpetual calendar Toric houses the automatic-winding PF333.01 movement with 45 hours of power reserve. It beats at 28,800 vibrations per hour, features 32 jewels and a double-spring barrel. The watch's functions include hours, minutes, seconds, precise moonphase display, and perpetual calendar with apertures for day, retrograde date, month and leap year. It is crafted in 18-karat white or rose gold and there is a gemstone version that is set with 60 baguette-cut Top Wesselton VVS diamonds weighing 3.8 carats. A distinct feature of this watch is the double knurling.

PATEK PHILIPPE - PERPETUAL CALENDAR

Classically executed, this Perpetual Calendar is equipped with the Caliber 240 Q. Automatic, it beats at 21,600 vibrations per hour, is powered by an off-center, unidirectional winding 22-karat gold micro-rotor, and is visible through a sapphire crystal caseback. Due to the three calendar adjusters positioned via the lugs, the bracelet features a special mechanism on the first link—both sides—to house the extensions of the small adjustment pushers.

PATEK PHILIPPE - REF. 5039

The refined Clous de Paris pattern on the bezel characterizes this watch and is indicative of some models from the Calatrava collection. Its Caliber 240Q with Geneva Seal is provided with a perpetual-calendar module and it is the most classic and recognizable movement among those produced by Patek Philippe. Caliber 240Q is displayed through the caseback and shows an off-center 21-karat gold micro-rotor and the exclusive Gyromax balance.

PATEK PHILIPPE - REF. 5059

This self-winding movement with Geneva Seal (Patek Philippe Caliber 315 S-QR) offers date, day, month, four-year leap cycle and moonphase readout. The 126 module, displaying the retrograde date indication over an arc of approximately 240 degrees, is visible through the transparent caseback of the Officier case, provided with the typical hinged cover. Through the sapphire-crystal caseback it is possible to observe the components of Caliber 315 with its center 21-karat gold rotor engraved with the Calatrava lily-cross, a symbol of the firm and synonymous with high international prestige.

PATEK PHILIPPE - CHRONOGRAPH PERPETUAL CALENDAR REF. 3970E

This model's manual-winding movement with Geneva Seal (Patek Philippe Cal. CH 27-70 Q, CH 27-70 base + calendar module) offers perpetual calendar (date, day, month, four-year cycle, moonphase) and chronograph with two counters.

ROGER DUBUIS - GOLDENSQUARE

From the GoldenSquare family, this self-winding watch houses the RD5739 caliber and is characterized by an elegant, curved square case. The perpetual-calendar model shown here measures 40mm and is provided with a calendar plate for analog-digital displays. Large hands and Roman numerals dominate the dial on which an easy-to-read day ring appears with the moonphase window. The perpetual calendar indicates large day and month at 12:00, date at 4:00 and moonphase at 8:00.

ROGER DUBUIS - HOMMAGE

This self-winding movement with Geneva Seal and Bulletin de l'Observatoire (caliber RD5739, Lemania base + Roger Dubuis calendar module) offers day, date, four-year leap cycle and moonphase readout. The only perpetual-calendar movement used today for the Hommage collection, realized in two sizes (40mm and 37mm), it combines the basic caliber with a module featuring a digital display of day, month and four-year cycle.

ROGER DUBUIS - HOMMAGE CHRONO BI-RETROGRADE PERPETUAL CALENDAR

This manual-winding movement with Geneva Seal and Bulletin de l'Observatoire (Roger Dubuis caliber RD5632, thoroughly modified Lemania base + calendar module) features perpetual calendar (retrograde date and day, month, four-year cycle, week, moonphase) and chronograph. The Hommage collection, created in 1996, features watches whose water resistance is guaranteed up to 50 meters. This is the homage Roger Dubuis wanted to pay to the most classic of possible shapes—the one used for the first watches of the history—as well as to all the watchmakers of the past, both famous and unknown, who contributed to its improvement. The Bulletin de l'Observatoire represents a guarantee of working precision and bears witness to the particular accuracy and finish of all the components, tuning and regulation of each individual movement.

ROGER DUBUIS - GOLDENSQUARE SINGLE-PUSHER CHRONO

PERPETUAL CALENDAR

This self-winding movement (caliber RD57, base + calendar module) offers perpetual calendar (oversized date, day, month, four-year cycle, moonphase) and single-pusher chronograph. Two substantial novelties were introduced in this watch by Roger Dubuis: a new square-curved case shape, called GoldenSquare, and the adoption of a new 240-part movement designed and produced by the watchmaker. This caliber combines the functions of a single-pusher chronograph with those of a calendar displayed through windows. These functions are integrated by a moonphase display and the hand indication of a second 24-hour time zone, provided with a digital day/night indicator. Switching between digital readings is instantaneous.

Grand Complications

ROGER DUBUIS - MUCHMORE

The MuchMore collection, first presented in Spring 1999, is characterized by an elegant, curved rectangular case, presented in five sizes and as homage to the models of the 1920s. This oversized perpetual-calendar version houses the caliber RD5739 and measures almost 47mm in height. In addition to the perpetual-calendar model (provided with a mixed-display module), the MuchMore family includes a single-pusher chronograph, a bi-retrograde calendar and two time-only models with manual or automatic mechanical movements.

ROGER DUBUIS - MUCHMORE WINDOW PERPETUAL CALENDAR
REF. M34 5739 0 9.7A

Crafted in 18-karat gold, this Window Perpetual Calendar watch houses the RD57 mechanical self-winding caliber with 25 jewels and decorated with the Côtes de Genève pattern. The watch is adjusted in five positions, and marked with the Geneva Quality Hallmark. The MuchMore Window Perpetual Calendar offers day and month at 12:00, leap year at 3:00, date, and moonphase.

ROGER DUBUIS - SYMPATHIE A GUICHET

This self-winding movement with Geneva Seal and Bulletin de l'Observatoire (caliber RD5739, Lemania base + Roger Dubuis module) offers date, day, month, four-year cycle and moonphase. Mixed indications (i.e. analog and digital) are featured by the shaped model shown in the photograph—the first with a round dial and the other in the typical shape of the Sympathie case. This model, as are all creations signed by Roger Dubuis, is realized as a limited edition of 28 pieces for each case and dial version.

ROGER DUBUIS - SYMPATHIE BI-RETROGRADE

This self-winding movement with Geneva Seal and Bulletin de l'Observatoire (caliber RD5610, Lemania base + Roger Dubuis calendar module) features date, day, four-year leap cycle and moonphase readout The movement with five center hands uses the analog calendar plate with two retrograde hands, which for many years has characterized some models. Its new features consist of a 180-degree rotation of the module, the positioning of the retrograde hands at the dial center and the digital leap-year cycle display.

ROGER DUBUIS - SYMPATHIE BI-RETROGRADE

This self-winding movement with Geneva Seal and Bulletin de l'Observatoire (caliber RD 5772, Lemania base + Roger Dubuis calendar module) offers date, day, four-year leap cycle and moonphase readout. On the screw-on caseback, an aperture protected by a sapphire crystal (on whose internal surface Roger Dubuis's monogram is engraved) displays the movement. The watch is water resistant to 5atm and is realized as a limited edition of 28 pieces for each version.

VACHERON CONSTANTIN - REF. 43033

This watch's self-winding Caliber 1120 QP base + module offers date, day, four-year leap cycle and moonphase readout. It is offered in yellow gold and platinum. The full dial, crossed by a refined guilloché decoration with a small-wave pattern, houses the usual functions. Year and month are indicated by a single hand. The months are repeated four times, which means that the hand makes a complete rotation every 48 months: three regular-year cycles and one leap year.

VACHERON CONSTANTIN - MALTE CHRONOGRAPH PERPETUAL CALENDAR

This manual-winding movement (Vacheron Constantin Caliber 1141 QP, Lemania base + calendar module) offers perpetual calendar (date, day, month, four-year cycle, moonphase) and chronograph. The modifications Vacheron Constantin made to the basic movement, produced by Nouvelle Lemania and visible through the wicket hinged on the caseback, refer particularly to the shapes of some bridges, the personalized decorations and the addition of a perpetual-calendar module. The moonphase is indicated on a gold disc engraved by hand. For the indication of the four-year cycle (consisting of the three digits 3-6-5, indicating the normal year, and 3-6-6 for the leap year) the unusual window system is adopted here. Rectangular pushers and evident moldings on the lugs and bezel stress the complex design characterizing the Malte collection.

VACHERON CONSTANTIN - MALTE QP

This self-winding Vacheron Constantin Caliber 1261 QPR offers retrograde date, day, month, four-digit year and four-year cycle. The pride of the Malte collection, this model is characterized by a fan-shaped date and a four-digit year displays with an additional indication of the leap-year position. The 39mm case has large grooved lugs. A Malta Cross is engraved on the crown and on the hinged cover over a sapphire-crystal caseback. The silvered dial shows arabesque decorations and gold or platinum markers. The watch comes in a precious wooden box containing a pin used to actuate the four correctors.

VACHERON CONSTANTIN - MINUTE REPEATER PERPETUAL CALENDAR 1755QP

A proprietary Vacheron Constantin design, the 13" caliber features center hour and minute hands, two-position stem for winding and setting, and offers 40 hours of power reserve. Crafted in either 18-karat rose gold or platinum, the perpetual calendar offers hour, minute, date, day of week, month, moonphase, and takes into account leap years. The minute repeater features an open-worked decoration and strikes the hours, quarters and minutes on a pair of tiny hammers. The movement houses 30 jewels, and beats at a frequency of 18,000 vibrations per hour.

VACHERON CONSTANTIN - PERPETUAL CALENDAR RETROGRADE REF. 47031

By combining a perpetual calendar with a 31-day retrograde calendar, Vacheron Constantin reaches new heights. The 39mm case, crafted in either platinum or 18-karat rose gold, houses the 1126 QPR automatic movement and offers hours, minutes, perpetual calendar, day and month indications via hands. Current year and leap year are shown through a window. The retrograde crescent offers 31-day date and the movement beats at 28,800 vibrations per hour.

VACHERON CONSTANTIN - SAINT-GERVAIS

This complicated watch pushes the existing limits of the power reserve. A world-first with four barrels coupled with a regulator tourbillon and a perpetual calendar, the watch has 250 hours of power reserve. The 44mm platinum-cased timepiece houses the new Caliber 2250 with 410 parts. In addition to the gold hour and minute hands, two blued steel hands run over the silvered engine-turned gold dial in arcs at 3:00 and 9:00 to indicate the power reserve of the barrels. Only 55 pieces of this watch will be created.

VACHERON CONSTANTIN - TOUR DE L'ILE

Vacheron Constantin's master watchmakers invested more than 10,000 hours on research and development—almost two years—into this multi-complication. Only seven Tour de L'Ile watches will ever be created and each will house 834 individual parts and offer 16 complications that can be read off of a double-faced watch. The 47mm case houses the new Caliber 2750 with toubillon, minute repeater, moonphase, age of moon, perpetual calendar, second time zone, equation of time, sunrise, sunset, and sky chart. The watch was created in honor of the brand's 250th anniversary, celebrated in 2005.

Grand Complications

ZENITH GRANDE - CHRONOMASTER XXT QUANTIÈME PERPETUAL

With the El Primero movement at the heart of Grande ChronoMaster XXT Quantieme Perpetual, this watch is one of the most accurate mechanical chronographs in the world, beating at 36,000 vibrations per hour. Now, the watch is equipped with a perpetual calendar that keeps hours, minutes, date, day, month, year and leap year. The new El Primero caliber 4003 is equipped with nine hands and a pointer on the dial to indicate the many functions of the movement. The case measures 45mm in diameter and is crafted in 18-karat white or pink gold.

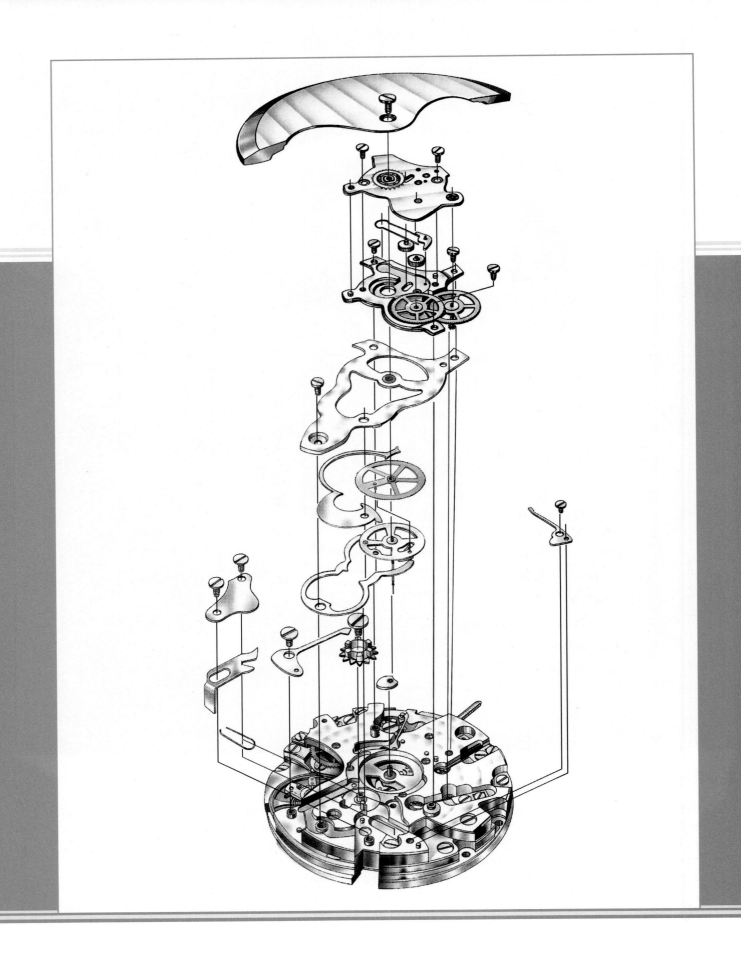

CHRONOGRAPHS, CHRONOGRAPH RATTRAPANTES AND FLYBACK

Volumes have been written about chronographs, their history and their development. While anything more than the basic timekeeping functions in a timepiece is considered a complication, the basic chronograph is so prevalent that it is not included herein. Instead, we focus on the complications built *upon* the basic chronograph: the flyback and the rattrapante.

Datograph movement.
The Datograph houses the manually wound caliber L951.1 flyback chronograph movement. It houses consists of 90 meticulously hand-finished parts with a frequency of 18,000 oscillations per hour.

The word "chronograph" is derived from the Greek words Chronos (time) and Grapho (I write), but "time writer" is the common translation. Essentially, a chronograph is a watch equipped with a device that also enables it to measure continuous or discontinuous intervals of time without affecting the time-telling functions. Often those intervals range from the tiniest fraction of a second up to 12 hours. Essentially, the wearer can push a button on the case to set in motion a separate hand, then stop it and return it to zero when the event has been timed.

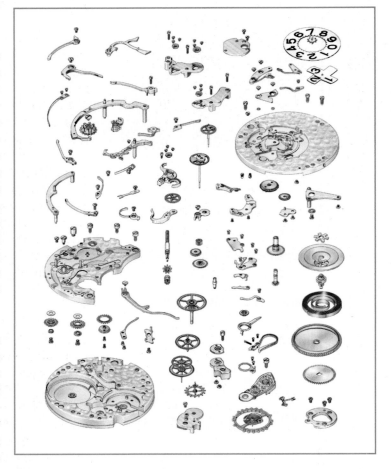

English watchmaker George Graham is generally credited with creating a mechanism in 1720 (though, not a watch) with weights and a pendulum that became the first device to measure small intervals of time. The hand of the mechanism divided the second into four segments. In 1821, Nicolas Rieussec invented the first true chronograph, which recorded intervals of time. The first chronograph clock was unveiled by Rieussec in 1822 and actually wrote the time to be measured on the clock dial. It had a hand constructed like a small pen that marked an ink spot directly on the dial at the beginning and at the end of the measuring process. The distance between the two dots represented the time that passed between starting and stopping.

Rieussec's invention set the world's watchmakers on a race to further perfect the chronograph. Hundreds of designs and patents in chronograph technology emerged. The goal was to perfect the movement so that the time-measurement function could run independently of the timekeeping functions to ensure maximum precision of both functions. Around the same time, Breguet and Fatton created a similar ink counter.

In 1840, Swiss horologist Adolphe Nicole, living in England, registered a patent for a device that allowed the user set the seconds hand back to zero—thereby introducing the

three functions of the modern day chronograph (start, stop and return to zero). It was not until 1862, though, that Nicole, working with Henri-Féréol Piquet, exhibited a chronograph that could start, stop and reset to zero without disturbing the clockwork mechanism. Eight years later in 1870, Joseph Winnerl of Paris introduced the first forerunner of today's split-second chronograph in a pocket watch. His watch featured two seconds hands, one on top of the other. One indicated the start of the action and the other marked the end.

With the turn of the century and the evolution of the wristwatch, it was just a matter of time before the chronograph made its way to the wrist. In fact, by 1913 the Omega watch company had already advertised a chronograph wristwatch, immediately followed by brands such as Movado, Heuer, Rolex and Ulysse Nardin—all offering wristwatch chronographs with the start, stop and return-to-zero functions achieved by a single pushpiece in the winding crown. In 1934 Breitling first advertised a wrist chronograph design with two pushbuttons on the case. One button would start and stop the chronograph as often as desired and the other moved the hand back to zero after the timing was stopped. This new mechanism quickly became a standard of chronographs and was adopted by a majority of other watchmaking firms. In 1969, an alliance between Heuer, Hamilton-Buren and Breitling resulted in the automatic chronograph.

Today's chronographs are easily recognizable because they typically have small subdials to track and total elapsed minutes and hours. Both manual- and automatic-winding chronographs exist.

Flyback chronographs and split-second chronographs—often referred to as rattrapantes and foudroyantes—are the hybrid versions of chronographs. Considered a complication within a complication, these movements are created by only the finest brands and enjoy prestige among the public.

First developed in the 1930s, the flybacks and chronograph rattrapantes were World War II projects aimed to improve

Chronographs, Chronograph Rattrapantes and Flyback

synchronization for specific functions and missions. Brands such as Zenith, Breitling and Longines led the developments. Breitling patented a two-pusher chronograph in 1933 and 1935, and Longines registered a patent in 1936 for the predecessor of today's flyback watch. The Longines piece was a two-pusher chronograph that, when the second pusher was pressed down during a timing operation, it reset the chronograph to zero; when released, the second hand started running again automatically.

Essentially, the flyback function is a fast-return feature without stopping. When the chronograph is started, one push of a button will return it to zero without stopping and immediately start running again. (With a regular chronograph, the wearer must stop the timing hand and then, when it returns to zero, press another button to start timing again.) The flyback chronograph is equipped with one sweep hand to do the timing.

A chronograph rattrapante or split-second chronograph is equipped with two sweep hands so that, when one starts the chronograph, both hands begin timing. Each hand can be stopped independently and one hand can catch up to the other. This function enables timing of several events of different duration simultaneously—all by pressing a single pusher and without stopping, zeroing and restarting the entire mechanism manually.

Over the years, hundreds of different chronograph rattrapantes have been developed. Some offer telemeter scales to measure distances, others feature tachometers to measure speeds, pulsimeters to measure pulse frequency, and altimeters to measure altitude. Many chronographs also offer calendars or moonphase indication. Those that are also equipped with the perpetual calendar are considered among the most technically advanced chronographs.

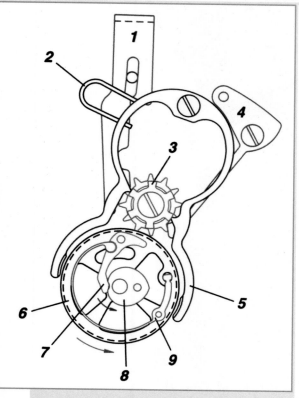

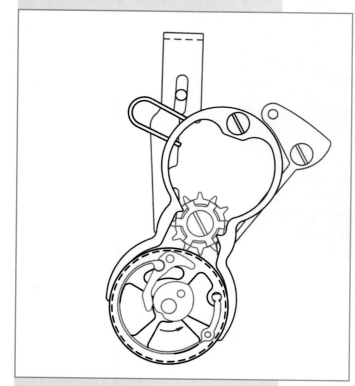

In the past few decades, advancements have come in the form of the column-wheel chronograph, and most recently, we have witnessed the unveiling of the Double Split Chronograph, first by A. Lange & Söhne and then by IWC.

A chronograph can also be a chronometer, however the terms should not be used interchangeably. Any timepiece—not just a chronograph—may be enrolled in testing for chronometer status.

Chronometers

A chronometer is a precision instrument whose movement is built to endure extreme conditions. Typically, a chronometer has undergone rigorous testing over a period of time in several positions and under different conditions and is found to meet certain criteria either by the watch brand building it or by a testing observatory. Most countries do not require certification for a watch to be called a chronometer.

In Switzerland, however, in order for a watch to be deemed a certified chronometer, it must endure stringent testing at the Controle Official Suisse des Chronometres (COSC).

At the COSC, the watch movement is exposed to tests that confirm water resistance, shock resistance, and accuracy under temperature and pressure extremes. To be certified when exposed to temperature change, for instance, a chronometer wristwatch cannot vary in accuracy more than plus or minus 0.6 seconds per day. Typically, the watch movement is tested for at least 15 days and is judged by unyielding standards that are set with absolute limits (calculations cannot be rounded off). If the watch passes these tests, it is officially certified as having achieved chronometer status. While there are several testing institutes, the most sought-after certificate is from the COSC.

A. LANGE & SÖHNE - 1815 CHRONOGRAPH

The 1815 Chronograph is created in either 18-karat white or pink gold and houses the manually wound caliber L951.0 movement with pulsimeter scale. The watch measures individual laps and cumulative times from 1/5th of a second to 30 minutes. It is equipped with a precise jumping minute counter and with flyback function, hours, minutes and small seconds with stop seconds. The 36-hour power-reserve movement consists of 320 parts and 34 jewels and features a lever escapement.

A. LANGE & SÖHNE - DATOGRAPH

A benchmark in the construction of superb mechanical chronographs, A. Lange & Söhne's Datograph houses the manually wound caliber L951.1 chronograph movement with a frequency of 18,000 oscillations per hour and consisting of 90 meticulously hand-finished parts. The watch features a precise jumping minute counter with a stepped pinion, flyback mechanism, column-wheel chronograph and Lange outsized date with rapid date adjustment. The flyback mechanism allows the user to reset the chronograph hands to zero during an ongoing time measurement and to start a new measurement simply by releasing the pushpiece again, thereby eliminating the stop, reset and restart action.

A. LANGE & SÖHNE - THE LANGE DOUBLE SPLIT

This model features two rattrapante hands: one for the seconds and one for the minutes to be stopped. The chronograph and rattrapante hands are flyback hands. With the Lange Double Split, comparative lap measurements of up to 30 minutes are possible for the first time. A. Lange & Söhne has filed for a patent for the disengagement mechanism that allows the chronograph sweep seconds hand to continue revolving while the rattrapante sweep seconds hand is stopped. A true technological achievement, the watch is also equipped with a balance wheel (developed in-house) equipped with poising weights instead of inertia screws. The balance spring is not attached to a hairspring stud, but instead is secured by a balance-spring clamp for which a separate patent registration has been filed. The manually wound, 465-part caliber L001.1 has 40 jewels.

Grand Complications

A. LANGE & SÖHNE - THE LANGE DOUBLE SPLIT MOVEMENT

The A. Lange & Söhne caliber L001.1 manually wound movement is precision adjusted in five positions and features plates and bridges made from untreated cross-laminated German silver. It houses 465 parts and 40 jewels, and is the world's first flyback chronograph with double rattrapante, controlled by classic column wheels. Other functions include jumping chronograph minute counter and rattrapante minute counter, flyback function, disengagement mechanism, hours, minutes, small seconds with stop seconds, power-reserve indicator, tachometer scale, and lap-time measurements between 1/6th of a second and 30 minutes.

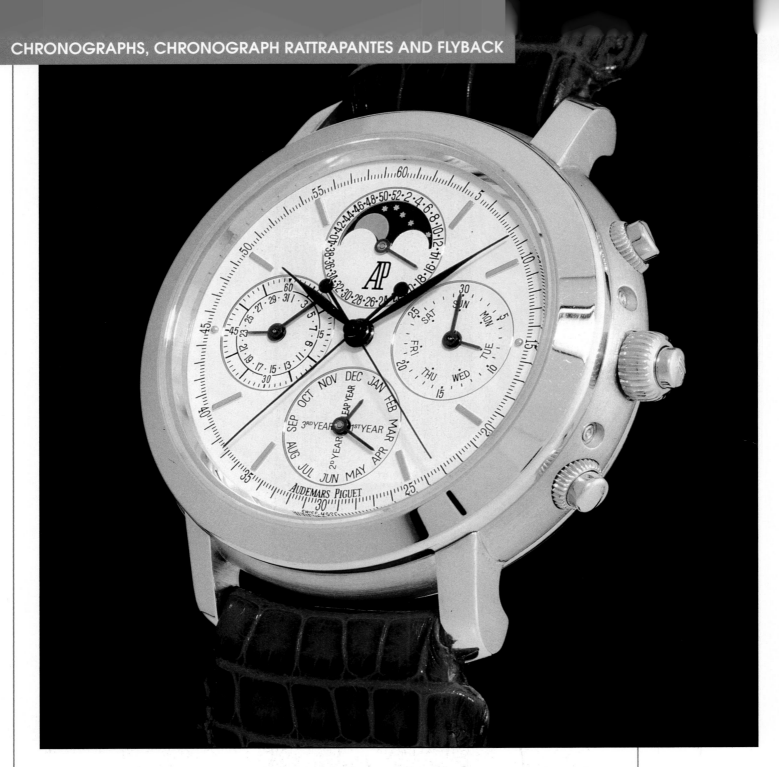

AUDEMARS PIGUET - JULES AUDEMARS GRANDE COMPLICATION

REF. 258660R

The Jules Audemars Grande Complication houses the self-winding caliber 2885 with more than 600 components. The watch offers perpetual calendar, minute repeater, and split-second chronograph. It is housed in 18-karat pink gold and features five correctors and a slide for the repeater on the side. The month and four-year cycle are positioned at 6:00 and the moonphase and date are shown at 12:00. This watch is also available in platinum.

AUDEMARS PIGUET - ROYAL OAK OFFSHORE

This self-winding Audemars Piguet Caliber 2226/2840 houses a chronograph with three counters, tachometer scale and date. The main parts of the solid case (bezel, middle and back, 61 components in total) are held together by eight screws and nuts in white gold. The inside space houses the movement insulated from magnetic fields by a soft-iron shield. The crowns and pushers are protected by rubber covers and the entire piece is finished by hand. About twenty operations are needed for simply the first mounting stage. Water resistance is guaranteed up to 10atm, made possible by complex technical solutions, among which are the use of Therban gaskets and the screwed closure of caseback and crown.

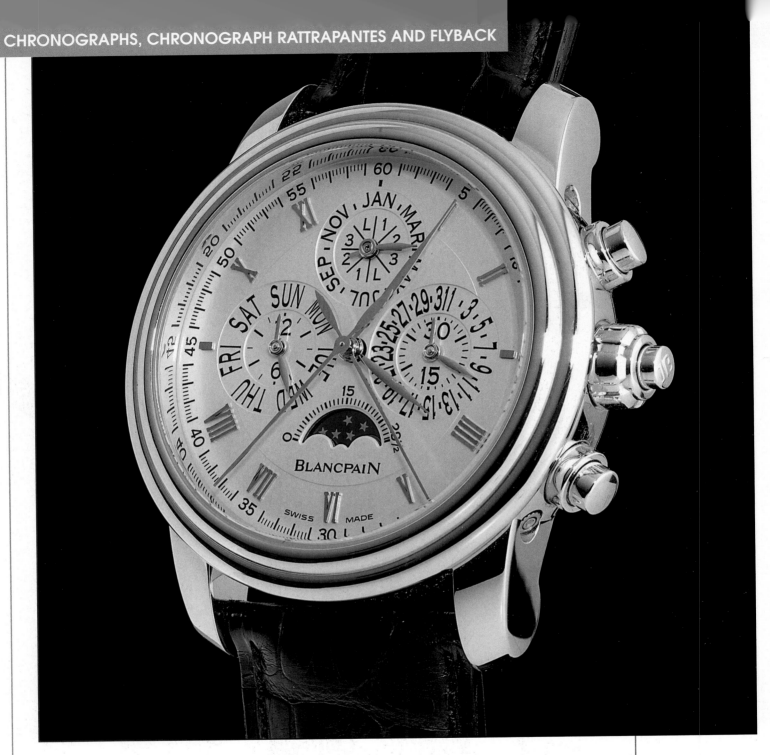

BLANCPAIN - LE BRASSUS PERPETUAL CALENDAR CHRONOGRAPH

This self-winding Blancpain caliber 56P9U (1185 base + 56QP module) offers perpetual calendar (date, day, month, four-year cycle and moonphase readout), and flyback split-second chronograph. This limited-edition model has a platinum case and closed back in an extra-large size (42mm). On the opaline dial, calendar and chronograph information appears in an analog big-size display assuring the best possible readability. The chronograph is provided with an additional split-second hand.

BREGUET - TYPE XX TRANSATLANTIQUE

This self-winding movement (caliber 582Q, Lemania caliber 1354 base) features a flyback chronograph with three counters. Breguet's Transatlantique adds a digital date display positioned at 6:00 to the general features of the Type XX. The basic caliber (13''' 3/4) was modified so as to realize the flyback function and to bring the minute-totalizing system up to 15. The watch is produced with a case in stainless steel, titanium and (yellow, pink or white) gold and various matching dial colors with applied Arabic numerals and luminescent Sport hands.

BREITLING - NAVITIMER OLYMPUS

This self-winding Breitling caliber 19 (ETA 2892A2 base + Kelek chronograph and calendar modules) offers a calendar preset for 4 years, and chronograph with three counters. Like all Breitling mechanical chronographs, this model is a COSC-certified chronometer. The only manual correction required for this four-year calendar watch is on March 1 of a leap year, i.e. every 1461 days. In addition to the slide-rule mounted on every Navitimer—allowing multiplications, divisions and proportions—this model features a scale for conversions of weights, measures and capacities on the caseback and is water resistant up to 3atm.

DE BETHUNE - SPLIT-SECONDS CHRONOGRAPH, PERPETUAL CALENDAR CS1

This split-seconds chronograph, minute-counter, and perpetual calendar with large date is a complicated watch offering exceptional legibility. It is the first watch in the De Bethune line to be fitted with a perpetual calendar and large date function. Crafted in 18-karat rose gold, the watch is 42mm in diameter and features an octagonal crown with included pusher for the split-seconds function. The 294-part movement features a Swiss lever escapement and 27 jewels, offers 30 hours of power reserve and is decorated with the Côtes de Genève pattern. The watch features hours and minutes, split-seconds chronograph, 30-minute counter at 3:00, month at 6:00, subseconds at 9:00, and date at 12:00. Winding and time setting are adjusted by the crown in two positions.

EBERHARD & CO. - TAZIO NUVOLARI RATTRAPANTE

In the limited series dedicated to the Italian Tazio Nuvolari, the fastest driver of his time, the Rattrapante is most impressive. Its striking case houses a Valjoux 7750 caliber modified by Eberhard, with the chronograph section operated by three comfortable rectangular pushers for the start, split, stop, restart, rattrapante and zero functions. The bezel is decorated with a circular graining pattern, the most used in mechanics in the first half of the twentieth century. An engraved black scale gives facilities for the average speed calculation (in miles) on a one-minute base. An alternative tachometric scale (in kilometers) is printed on the dial just under the bezel. To bring luck to the driver, a turtle carapace is represented at 12:00.

FRANCK MULLER - CINTRÉE CURVEX CHRONOGRAPH BI-RETROGRADE
PERPETUAL CALENDAR

This self-winding movement (FM 5888 BR, Franck Muller 7000 base + Dubois Dépraz exclusive calendar module) offers perpetual calendar (retrograde date and day, month, four-year cycle, moonphase) and chronograph with three counters. It is equipped with an automatic movement with 950 platinum rotor and a chronograph time display up to 12 hours and 30 minutes. The guilloché dial, covered by a translucent enamel layer, with silvered subdials and mother-of-pearl inlays, displays the original retrograde indications of the day of the week and date. Leap year is indicated digitally and shares its position at 12:00 with the month hand.

Chronographs, Chronograph Rattrapantes and Flyback

FRANCK MULLER - CINTRÉE CURVEX CHRONOGRAPH PERPETUAL CALENDAR

This self-winding movement (Franck Muller caliber. 7000 + Dubois Dépraz calendar module) offers perpetual calendar (date, day, retrograde month, four-year cycle, moonphase) and chronograph with one counter. The model was first created in 1999 and is characterized by the basic movement (a self-winding chronograph with a platinum rotor) as well as the exclusive patented perpetual-calendar module, with a retrograde month hand and 24-hour subdial. The original dial setting features a circular sexagesimal scale in two colors and showing divisions for 1/5 of a second. The caseback is guilloché, while the ring with the typical Arabic numerals is brushed.

FRANCK MULLER - CINTREE CURVEX MASTER BANKER

This self-winding movement (Franck Muller caliber 7000 MB) offers chronograph with two counters and triple time-zone indication. The watch is based on a single adjustment system controlled by the crown. In this large-size model (whose case measures 40.7x35mm) the Master Banker adds the chronograph, which seemed impossible to combine with the additional module for the GMT indication. To make it possible, it was necessary to develop a patented locking system of the different functions that would allow actuating the chronograph without interfering with the components of the plate dedicated to the additional time-zone indications.

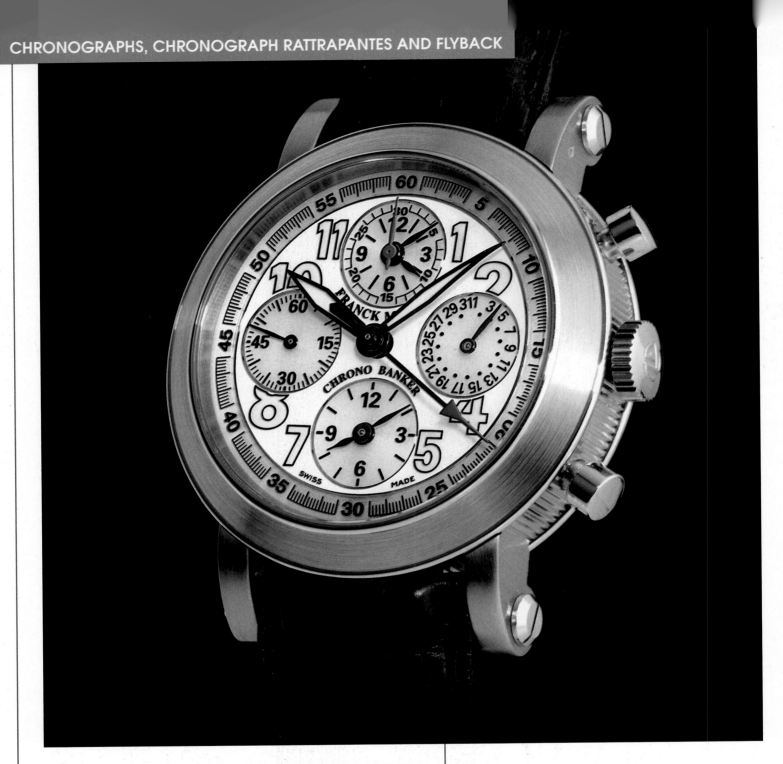

FRANCK MULLER - RONDE MASTER BANKER

This self-winding movement (Franck Muller caliber 7000 MB, Valjoux 7750 base) offers chronograph with two counters and triple time-zone indication. To realize this watch it was necessary to completely redesign the movement's pillar-plate by integrating the chronograph gears with those dedicated to the triple time-zone function, which can be adjusted by the crown.

GIRARD-PERREGAUX - G.P. POUR FERRARI "F310B" CHRONOGRAPH PERPETUAL CALENDAR

This self-winding Girard-Perregaux caliber 3170 (3100 base + calendar and chronograph modules) offers perpetual calendar (date, day, month on four-year cycle, moonphase), chronograph with three counters and tachometer scale. The affinities existing between Girard-Perregaux and Ferrari are brought to life in the titanium model dedicated to the F1 "F310B" and bear witness to the brands' shared will to overcome and control technology, materials and shapes in their respective extreme expressions. The dial is carbon fiber, an advanced material often used in the aeronautic and automotive industries, especially for race cars.

Chronographs, Chronograph Rattrapantes and Flyback

GIRARD-PERREGAUX - S.F. FOUDROYANTE

The S.F. Foudroyante's self-winding Girard-Perregaux caliber 8020 offers chronograph with three counters (60 second, 30 minute, eighths of a second) and is water resistant up to 3atm. The originality of this mechanism, very complex even at its basic level, consists of the foudroyante hand indicating the eighths of a second on a subdial positioned at 9:00.

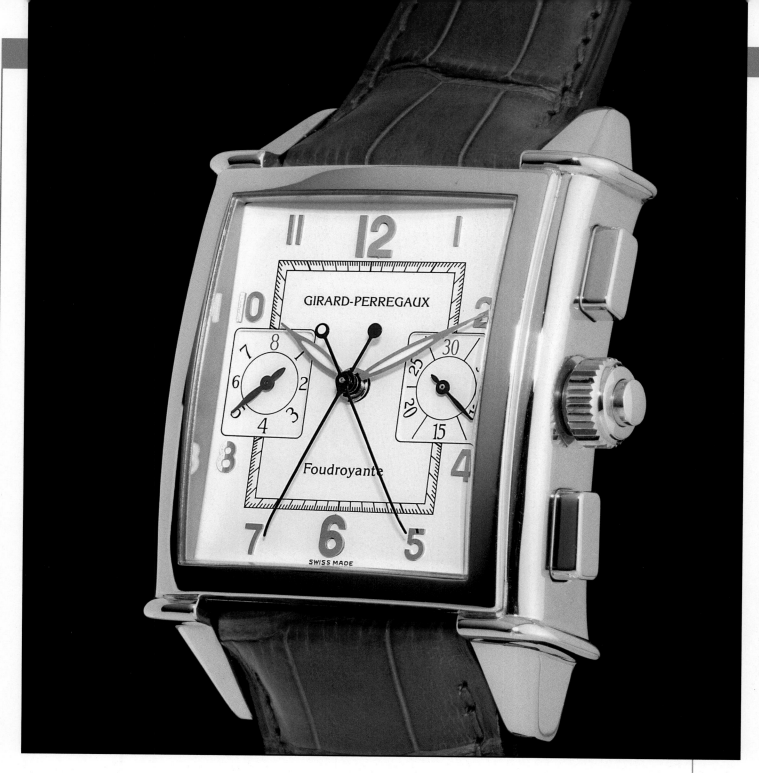

GIRARD-PERREGAUX - VINTAGE 1945 XXL SPLIT-SECOND CHRONOGRAPH

REF. 90210

Complete with jumping seconds, this automatic Vintage 1945 XXL Split-Second Chronograph houses the GP 604C0 movement with 60 jewels and 42 hours of power reserve. Based on the Valjoux caliber 7750, the watch features three chronograph counters: 60-seconds, 30-minutes and eighths of a second. Water resistant to 30 meters, the Vintage 1945 XXL Split-Second Chronograph beats at 28,800 vibrations per hour and features a sapphire caseback with four screws.

GLASHÜTTE ORIGINAL - PANORETROGRAPH

The PanoRetroGraph's manual-winding movement (Glashütte Original caliber 60) with flyback chronograph exhibits a 30-minute sector-type counter with a three-arm hand on its guilloché gold dial. A highly complex mechanism—controlled by the pusher positioned at 10:00—can revert the motion of the chronograph seconds and minute hands for the (30-minute) countdown function with a final acoustic sound (produced by a hammer striking an annular wire gong). The balance is provided with compensating screws, jewels are housed in screwed-on gold sets and the micrometer-screw regulation system has a swan-neck draw-back spring.

GLASHÜTTE ORIGINAL - PANOGRAPH

This PanoGraph's manual-winding movement (Glashütte Original caliber 61) with flyback chronograph and oversized date is a direct descendant of the PanoRetroGraph. The PanoGraph model adopts the same arrangement of the indications displayed on the dial: off-center hours and minutes, small seconds at 8:00, oversized panoramic date display, in-line second and minute totalizers, the latter on a concentric circle-sector scale. With respect to the caliber 60, this derived movement does not feature the countdown function; but its technical characteristics—such as its classical column-wheel construction and the flyback mechanism—are the same. Elegant engravings are realized by hand on the pillar-plate and movement bridges. The 41-jeweled movement is displayed through the caseback.

IWC - DA VINCI RATTRAPANTE 3754

The sophisticated Da Vinci Rattrapante houses the mechanical chronograph movement caliber 79252 with 43 jewels and 44 hours of power reserve. The watch offers perpetual calendar and perpetual moonphase indicator, as well as a split-second hand for intermediate timing.

IWC - SPITFIRE DOUBLE CHRONOGRAPH 3713

This mechanical double chronograph offers a split-second hand for intermediate timing, day/date indication and small second hand. It features a soft iron inner case to protect against magnetic fields and houses the caliber 79230 with 29 jewels and 44 hours of power reserve. Spitfire Double Chronograph 3713 beats at 28,800 vibrations per hour.

RICHARD MILLE - RM 004 SPLIT-SECOND CHRONOGRAPH

The RM 004 is a revolutionary movement that offers split-second chronograph and power reserve. Developed by Mille in conjunction with Renaud Papi, the movement features a modified escapement that reduces the friction and offers more effective shock absorption than its predecessors. Crafted in titanium, the RM 004 Split-Second Chronograph offers a torque-intercepting device and 72 hours of power reserve.

RICHARD MILLE - RM 008 TOURBILLON CHRONOGRAPH

Housing a manual-winding mechanism, this watch offers hour, minute, 70 hours of power reserve, torque indicator, split-second chronograph and function indicator. The column-wheel chronograph is crafted of titanium, and is operated by pressing the pusher at 8:00. The watch features a variable inertia balance wheel and a fast-rotating barrel (6 hours per revolution instead of 7.5 hours). It features a bottom plate and center bridge of titanium. The watch is offered in titanium or gold.

Chronographs, Chronograph Rattrapantes and Flyback

ZENITH - CHRONOMASTER EL PRIMERO MOONPHASE

This ChronoMaster's self-winding chronometer movement (Zenith El Primero 41.0) chronograph with three counters features a tachometer scale, full calendar (date, day, month) and moonphase. The El Primero 41.0 caliber is Zenith's only currently produced self-winding movement, a COSC-certified chronometer provided with a balance working at the frequency of 36,000 vibrations per hour that assures an accuracy of 1/10 second. The watch is produced in stainless steel and in yellow or pink gold with a leather strap or bracelet, or in platinum with a leather strap. The diamond version features a bezel studded with 144 set diamonds, diamond markers, and has a diameter of 40 or 43mm. The movement, provided with a guilloché white-gold rotor, is displayed through the transparent caseback protected by a hinged cover. The strap is crocodile leather.

ZENITH - GRAND CHRONOMASTER GT

This Grand ChronoMaster GT's self-winding chronometer movement (Zenith El Primero 40.01) flyback chronograph with three counters features a tachometer scale, full calendar (date, day, month), and moonphase. The ChronoMaster collection celebrated the 100th anniversary of Zenith's foundation and is equipped with an exceptional caliber, enriched 40 years later by models provided with a flyback device. The first one, the Grand ChronoMaster GT, houses the new 40.01 caliber in a 41mm case, larger than the traditional case.

Chronographs, Chronograph Rattrapantes and Flyback

ZENITH – GRAND CHRONOMASTER XT

The 43mm case of the Grand ChronoMaster XT model has even larger sizes and is equipped with the 40.09 chronometer caliber—a further evolution of the famed El Primero—with flyback feature. It also offers analog moonphase readout via a hand that shares the subdial positioned at 6:00 with the hour counter. The case displays the precious mechanism through its sapphire-crystal back.

ZENITH - GRAND CLASS RATTRAPANTE GRANDE DATE

The Grande Class Rattrapante Grande Date is powered by Zenith's El Primero and features big date at 6:00 and the split-second chronograph function.

RETROGRADES AND JUMP HOURS

A jumping hour watch derives its name from a device in which the hour digit instantly "jumps" into view via a one- or two-window aperture. This jumping hour method has progressed so that some manufacturers offer jumping minutes and jumping dates, as well. In a similar vein, retrograde readouts display time in an arc, usually one of 180 degrees. When the hand reaches the end of the arc, it automatically jumps back to the beginning and continues tracking time.

Typically, the jump-hour system works via a rotating-disc process. J. Pallweber developed the concept further in 1882 and created a jumping-hour and -minute watch with two separate windows. It was a popular complication for pocket watches through-out the late 19th and early 20th centuries. Today, it is a particularly sophisticated look for wristwatches.

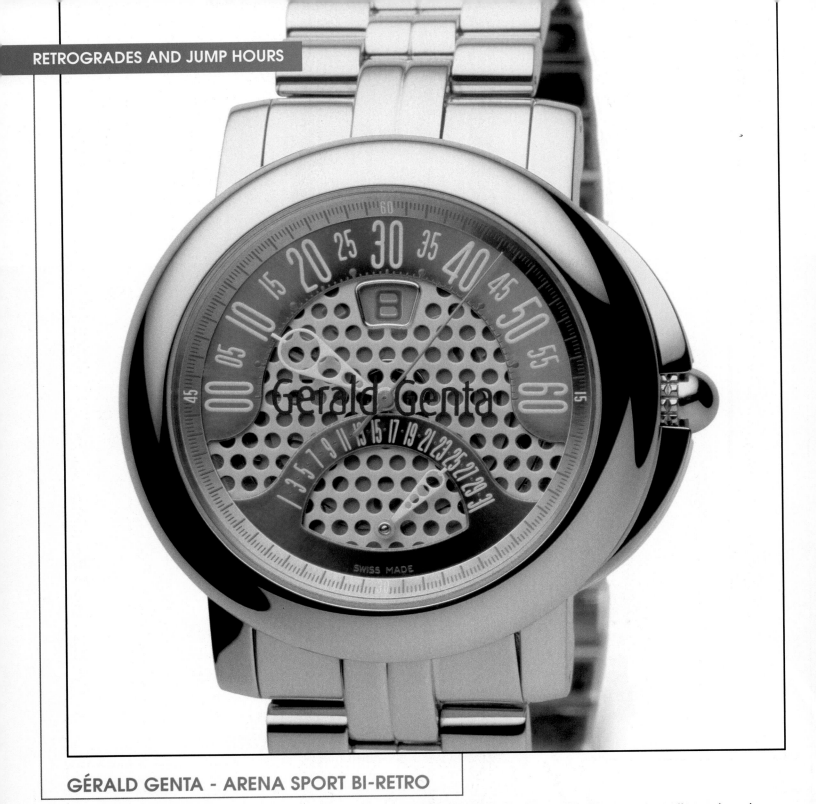

GÉRALD GENTA - ARENA SPORT BI-RETRO

The Arena Sport Bi-Retro has a steel case with crown protector, blue net-like dial on an orange hour disc and steel bracelet. This watch is equipped with an automatic movement with jumping hour, retrograde minutes and date. It has 42 hours of power reserve and the case is water resistant up to 3atm.

GÉRALD GENTA - ARENA CONTEMPORARY BI-RETRO

From the Arena Contemporary collection, this Bi-Retro has a steel case, blue Fabergé-style guilloché dial and dark blue alligator strap. This watch is equipped with an automatic movement with jumping hours, retrograde minutes and date. It has 42 hours of power reserve and the case is water resistant up to 3atm.

GÉRALD GENTA - OCTO BI-RETRO REF. OBR.Y.50.510.CN.BD

The OCTO Bi-Retro has a white-gold octagonal case and black-and-red lacquer dial. It is equipped with an automatic movement with jumping hours, retrograde minutes and date. The watch offers 45 hours of power reserve, and is water resistant to 10atm.

Grand Complications

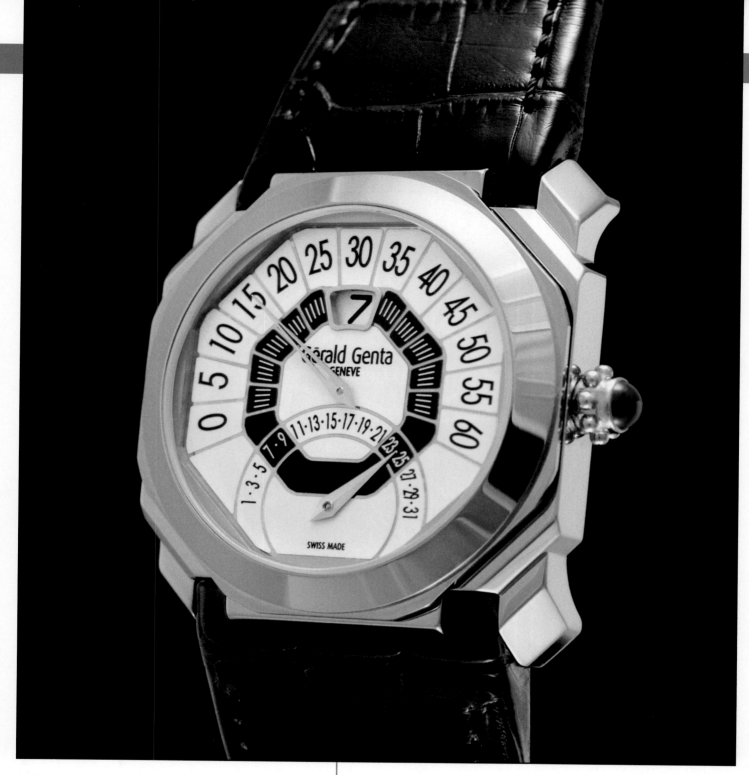

GÉRALD GENTA - OCTO BI-RETRO

From the OCTO collection, the OCTO Bi-Retro has a white-gold octagonal case, black and white lacquer dial and a black alligator strap. This watch is equipped with a Gérald Genta automatic movement with jumping hours, retrograde minutes and date. It has 45 hours power reserve and the case is water resistant up to 10atm.

GÉRALD GENTA - SPORT TOURBILLON RETROGRADE HOURS

From the Arena Sport collection, this 41mm watch is offered in platinum with a palladium bezel and a net-like black and steel dial. It is equipped with a tourbillon automatic movement (developed in-house) with a 240-degree retrograde hour with readout at 12:00. The tourbillon is visible at 6:00 and fixed with a sapphire bridge.

GIRARD-PERREGAUX - VINTAGE 1945 MAGISTRAL TOURBILLON REF. 99710

Housing the remontage manual-winding GP09700.3950 movement, this stunning Vintage 1945 Magisterial Tourbillon boasts astonishing features that delight both the eye and the ear. The Tourbillon with gold Bridge is visible through the dial aperture at 6:00; the retrograde date hand and the power-reserve indicator are offered on gold quarter-moon subdials. The watch also offers the delicate chiming of the time via a very refined striking mechanism. This model is water resistant to 30 meters and beats at a rate of 21,600 vibrations per hour.

HARRY WINSTON - AVENUE C JUMPING HOURS

The elegant Avenue C Jumping Hours embodies Harry Winston's constant zest for invention. The watch houses the manually wound HW315 movement that is a tonneau-shaped caliber to correspond to the case shape. A sapphire crystal caseback reveals the classical Côtes de Genève decoration. The watch is launched in platinum in a limited edition of 25 pieces with blue/silver dial and 25 pieces with ruthenium/silver dial. The jumping hour appears alone in the trapeze shaped aperture at 12:00. The Off-center dials for the minutes and give the way a daring look.

HARRY WINSTON - EXCENTER CHRONO

The Excenter Chrono features a triple-retrograde display of the chronograph functions by means of pointer-type displays. The 30-minute counter is at 4:00, the chronograph seconds is at 6:00 and the 12-hour counter is at 8:00. The hours and minutes are off-centered at 12:00. The mechanical self-winding Frédéric Piguet 1185 movement features a column-wheel chronograph with HW2831 module with compensating toothed wheel with no backlash to ensure greater precision of the hour and minute display. The case is 39mm and is crafted in 18-karat white or rose gold with a diamond-set version. Dials are anthracite or mother of pearl and the watch is water resistant to 30 meters.

HARRY WINSTON - EXCENTER TIMEZONE

The launch of the first Excenter timepiece by Harry Winston in 2002 ushered in a new generation of complicated watches for the brand. With off-center counters, this Excenter Timezone watch houses the Jacquet 7060 mechanical movement that enables a second time zone to be read off a 24-hour retrograde counter. It offers 5 days of power reserve, displayed at 12:00. The date aperture is at 6:00 and the hours and minutes are on the right side of the dial with a luminous day/night indicator below it. The second time zone is shown on a 24-hour retrograde counter on the left side of the dial. This distinctive watch uses a world-first compensating toothed gear with no backlash to ensure greater precision of the hour and minute display. The dial combines elegance and legibility. The 39mm watch is crafted in 18-karat white gold and is water resistant to 30 meters.

Grand Complications

HARRY WINSTON - PREMIER BIRETROGRADE

Designed in the New York studios and hand crafted and assembled by a master watchmaker in Switzerland, the Premier Biretrograde watch features an automatic movement consisting of 223 parts and 36 rubies. A double-retrograde module designed exclusively for Harry Winston has been adapted to work with the Girard-Perregaux GP3106 automatic movement. This outstanding watch features retrograde display of both seconds and the day of the week in two windows at 9:00 and 3:00 on the dial. The 35mm case is crafted in 18-karat white or yellow gold and is water resistant to 30 meters. The watch required fourteen months to make and features a sapphire caseback.

HARRY WINSTON - PROJECT Z1

Ronald Winston, who takes a very active role in the company's watchmaking business, has also unveiled a watch that he took particular interest in: the Project Z1. The new collection features a high-tech sports watch designed with three world firsts: an automatic chronograph with three off-center retrograde indicators; a radically different design; and a totally new material for watchmaking. Headed by Ronald Winston himself, the material for the Project Z1 watches is a rare alloy named Zalium for its major component, zirconium. Used in jet engines, Zalium had never been used in watchmaking because it is very hard and extremely difficult to work with. In fact, it must be very carefully machined from the ingot because the dust can catch fire. The Project Z1 watch is made in a limited edition of 100 pieces.

JAQUET DROZ - LES DOUZE VILLES EMAIL

Created in a limited edition of 88 pieces, this jumping hour and 12 time-zone watch houses the Jaquet Droz caliber 3663-4 self-winding mechanical movement with double barrels. The jumping hours are visible through an aperture at 12:00 and the 12 time zones are depicted through an aperture that displays 12 international cities' names. The 18-karat white-gold watch houses 28 jewels, offers 72 hours of power reserve, and is water resistant to 30 meters.

JAQUET DROZ - LES LUNES EMAIL

This unusual Jaquet Droz watch features a calendar with days and months through an aperture and a pointer-type date. It also features an interesting moonphase readout via a retrograde hand and five circular moon-depiction apertures. The watch houses the Jaquet Droz caliber 6553-4 self-winding mechanical movement with 28 jewels and beating at 28,800 vibrations per hour. The 40.5mm, 18-karat white-gold watch offers 72 hours of power reserve. Each piece is numbered individually and water resistant to 100 feet.

PARMIGIANI FLEURIER - TORIC RETROGRADE PERPETUAL CALENDAR

This perpetual calendar Toric houses the automatic-winding PF333.01 movement with 45 hours of power reserve. It beats at 28,800 vibrations per hour, features 32 jewels and a double-spring barrel. The watch's functions include hours, minutes, seconds, precise moonphase display, and perpetual calendar with apertures for day, retrograde date, month and leap year. It is crafted in 18-karat white or rose gold and there is a gemstone version that is set with 60 baguette-cut Top Wesselton VVS diamonds weighing 3.8 carats. A distinct feature of this watch is the double knurling.

PIAGET - EMPERADOR RETROGRADE REF. GOA 28071

Piaget's most prestigious showcase for its mechanical movements, the Emperador now includes this retrograde seconds complication. The apparent simplicity of this dial conceals a highly complex mechanism. Every 30 seconds (2,880 times a day) this retrograde hand jumps suddenly, swiftly and accurately back from position 30 to position 0 and immediately resumes its onward course. The retrograde seconds hand on the Piaget Emperador is shown in a fan-shaped guilloché-worked segment at 12:00. On the opposite side is a large circular date window. At the heart of this prestigious creation is the automatic 560P caliber. Designed and developed by Piaget, this movement oscillates at a frequency of 21,600 vibrations per hour, offers 40 hours of power reserve and houses 29 jewels.It provides indications of the hours, minutes and date at 6:00, as well as the retrograde seconds at 12:00.

PIERRE KUNZ - CARRÉE TRIPLE RETROGRADE SECONDS

This model is a unique virtuosity in the flyback arena. The continuous seconds function is now divided into three individual counters of twenty seconds each; the three hands flyback into position after their respective twenty-second runs are completed and each "rests" for forty seconds before a new start. The white-gold 37mm square variation of the typical Pierre Kunz case houses an automatic-winding PKA 2001-base caliber combined with the 2327 module. Two structural versions are available for the dial; the three sectors can be engine-turned or open to reveal the decorated module below.

ROGER DUBUIS - COLLECTION GOLDENSQUARE THREE RETROGRADE

REF. G40 5799 5 GN 1.6A

With a mother-of-pearl guilloché dial, this GoldenSquare features a dragging and retrograde minute, jumping and retrograde date. It houses the three-retrograde caliber 5799 with 11-1/2 lignes and 27 jewels. The self-winding movement is adjusted in five positions. Only 28 pieces are being created.

ZENITH - CHRONOMASTER OPEN RETROGRADE

The 950 platinum ChronoMaster Open is powered by the automatic chronograph movement, 13''' caliber El Primero 4023. The movement (Ø 30x7.75mm high with 299 parts) beats at 36,000 vph, has 50-hour autonomy, measures to 1/10th of a second and features a 22-karat white-gold guilloché oscillating weight with Grain d'Orge pattern. The piece features an open dial at 10:00 displaying El Primero, white-gold appliqué numerals, center hour and minute, small seconds at 9:00, 30-minute counter at 3:00, retrograde date indicator from 30-minute axis, power-reserve indicator from hour axis (with pink-gold hand). Mounted on black, hand-stitched alligator strap lined with silky Alzavel calfskin, with 18-karat white-gold ChronoMaster triple-folding buckle stamped with Zenith Star.
T version: Ø 40 mm / opening: Ø 29.9 mm
XXT version: Ø 45 mm opening: Ø 35 mm.

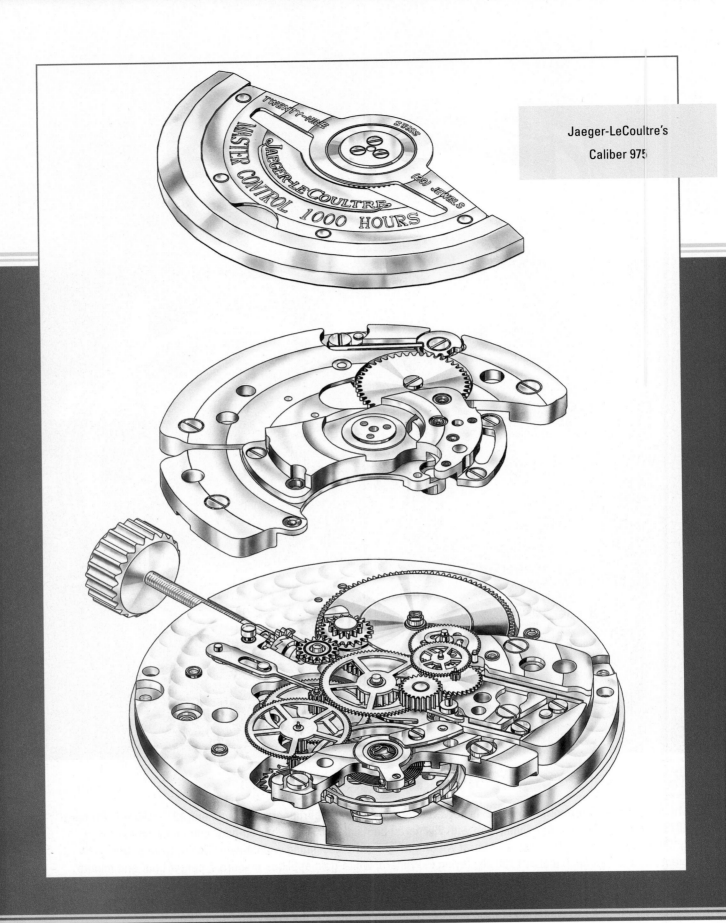

Grand Complications

Multiple Time Zones and GMTs

Savvy watchmakers keep pace with the ever changing times and lifestyle demands of their clients by anticipating their needs and developing technologies to answer their demands. Among the complications being implemented regularly in many fine wristwatches are dual and triple time zones, GMT and world time readouts.

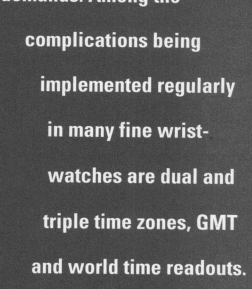

Because business is conducted every day via computers, which allow for virtual instantaneous communication anywhere in the world, having the time-zone differences at one's fingertips is critical. Because they answer an immediate need, multiple time-zone watches have become one of the watch industry's most popular tools.

At the dawn of time, the sun was the only indicator by which to estimate time. When it was directly overhead, it was noon. As the world's people began to traverse the oceans, it became more and more important to recognize the existence of different time zones.

In 1883, standard time was fixed to prevent the differences of time that resulted in different localities depending on the longitudes of the place. At every 15 degrees longitude on the map, lines were drawn to create 24 different international time zones. Each zone differs from the preceding and following zone by one hour. By referring to a map and making minimal calculations, seafarers and other adventurous travelers could calculate time differences, although these differences were of little significance to them at that time because travel was slow and communication was not instantaneous. As the pace of travel quickened and technology advanced, watch companies recognized the need to make the time-zone changes more accessible.

Until recently, most dual time-zone watches featured either two faces on the main dial, a subdial on the main dial, or reversible dials. Recent technology has allowed for more adventurous design, bringing forth the hidden hand, wherein the watch features traditional hour, minute and second hands, and has another hour hand tucked away beneath.

To activate the second time-zone function, the wearer simply adjusts the lower hour hand, which is a different color than the others.

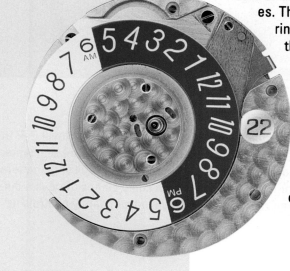

The lower hand is the second time-zone indicator. Typically, to activate the second time-zone function, the wearer simply adjusts the lower hour hand, which is a different color than the others. The watch functions automatically until the wearer no longer needs the second time zone and then hides the hand away again. (Some of these designs also offer an instant set button that allows the wearer to change the hour of the second time-zone hand without moving the main hands.)

Triple time-zone watches have also become a reality, often with the third zone being read off of a digital display window or the bezel, as is the case with many 24-hour watches. These tools of the trade typically feature a 24-hour ring as the outer bezel, which indicates the time in a third location. Also available are GMT or Universal Time watches that enable the wearer to calculate the time in any of the 24 time zones around the world. GMT is indicated in a variety of ways, depending on the manufacturer, and normally requires some calculation on the part of the wearer. But thanks to advanced technologies, today's wristwatches often feature indicators or prompts that make these additions or subtractions easy to calculate.

AUDEMARS PIGUET - ROYAL OAK DUAL TIME

This self-winding Audemars Piguet caliber 2129/2845 offers dual time on an additional dial. The Royal Oak Dual Time adopts a movement designed in 1989 and now shared by all the GMT watches of the brand. The case, water resistant up to 50atm, has a dial characterized by the modern look of a checkered Grande Tapisserie pattern. The second time zone is displayed at 6:00 by a double hand for hours and minutes (in some places there is a difference of about a quarter of an hour with respect to the home time zone) and the crown independently controls its regulation.

BLANCPAIN - LEMAN 2100 TIME ZONE

This self-winding Frédéric Piguet caliber 5L60 for Blancpain offers dual time on an additional dial with day/night indication. An extra-thin automatic movement drives Blancpain's Leman 2100 Time Zone model, whose water resistance is guaranteed up to 10atm. The dial's geometry is characterized by the upward off-center arrangement of the hour and minute display of the second time-zone indication, and by the presence of the relevant window for day/night indication. The crown controls all functions, including the date.

BLANCPAIN - LE BRASSUS QUANTIEME MOONPHASE GMT

This self-winding Frédéric Piguet caliber 67A6 for Blancpain features dual time with an independent center hand. From the Le Brassus collection, this model combines a full calendar (date, day of the week, month and moonphase) and the second time-zone display by an independent hand on a 24-hour basis. The movement consists of a self-winding 1151 caliber base and additional modules for full calendar and second time zone. The platinum case of Blancpain's Quantième Moonphase GMT is water resistant up to 5atm.

CHOPARD - L.U.C GMT

This self-winding Chopard caliber L.U.C 4.96/1-H1 (L.U.C 4.96 base) offers dual time on an additional dial with 24 hour and day/night indicator. Chopard's first GMT, equipped with movement made entirely in-house, is provided with a micro-rotor and two superimposed barrels (assuring an autonomy of 65 hours). This well refined mechanism, displayed through the caseback, obtained the COSC's chronometer-precision certificate. Other features are the digital date display at 3:00, the additional time visualized at 6:00 on a 24-hour subdial with day-night color divisions, decorated with a guilloché soleil pattern on the silvered section and a line pattern on the black section.

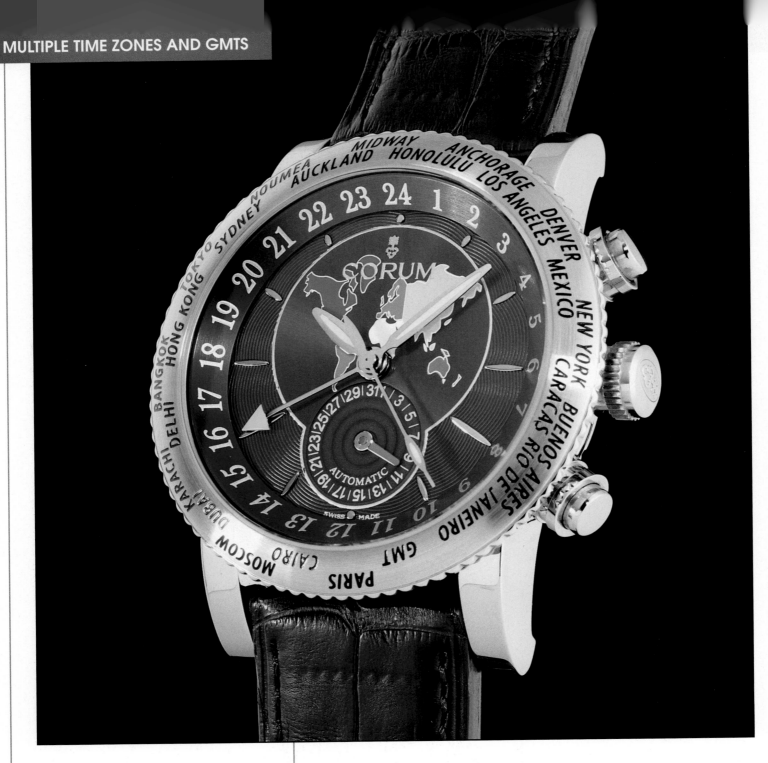

CORUM - CLASSICAL GMT

A classic World Timer "on demand" joins the dynamic Bubble GMT in the Corum collection. This COSC-certified chronometer houses a CO-983 automatic caliber showing the second time zone on a 24-hour scale via a central arrow-tipped hand. Manually rotating the bezel, according to the location, provides a contemporary view of the 24 time zones. An oversized case offers more room for the 24 cities, engraved in black on the bezel, and two big pushers allow the quick setting of the desired alternate hour/time zone.

DE BETHUNE - GMT POWER RESERVE

The new De Bethune brand maintains the most traditional values of Swiss horology with its classic esthetics and mechanical movements. It offers a GMT with a subdial for the second time-zone display and an independent white hand (the second hand, matching the color of the main hands, indicates the 24-hour reference). Below the three windows at 12:00, a disc with a blue background and a white indicator shows the power state (minimum/maximum). The barrel assures a power reserve of seven days. The crown controls all functions.

de GRISOGONO - DOPPIO TRE

The Doppio Tre watch from de Grisogono is crafted in 18-karat rose gold and shown here with alligator strap. It houses an automatic mechanical movement that offers large date aperture and three independent time-zone readouts. It is water resistant to 50 meters.

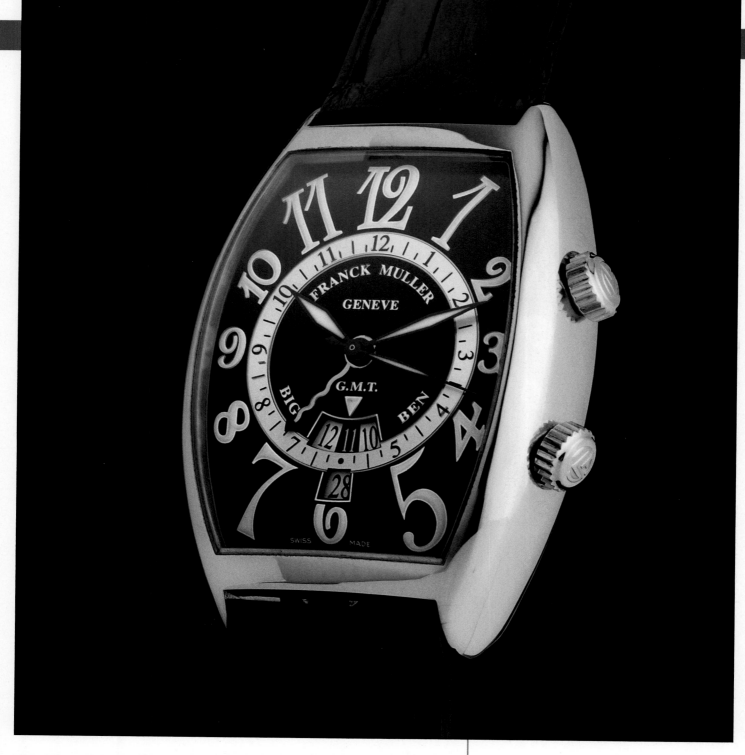

FRANCK MULLER - CINTRÉE CURVEX BIG BEN GMT

This self-winding Franck Muller caliber 7850 (base Girard-Perregaux caliber 2291) offers dual time through a 24-hour window. In this version, the second time-zone window and date display are positioned one above the other at 6:00. The alarm function is indicated by a small center hand and controlled by a second dedicated crown positioned at 4:00. The crown at 2:00 sets the main time, that of the second time zone, and winds the movement.

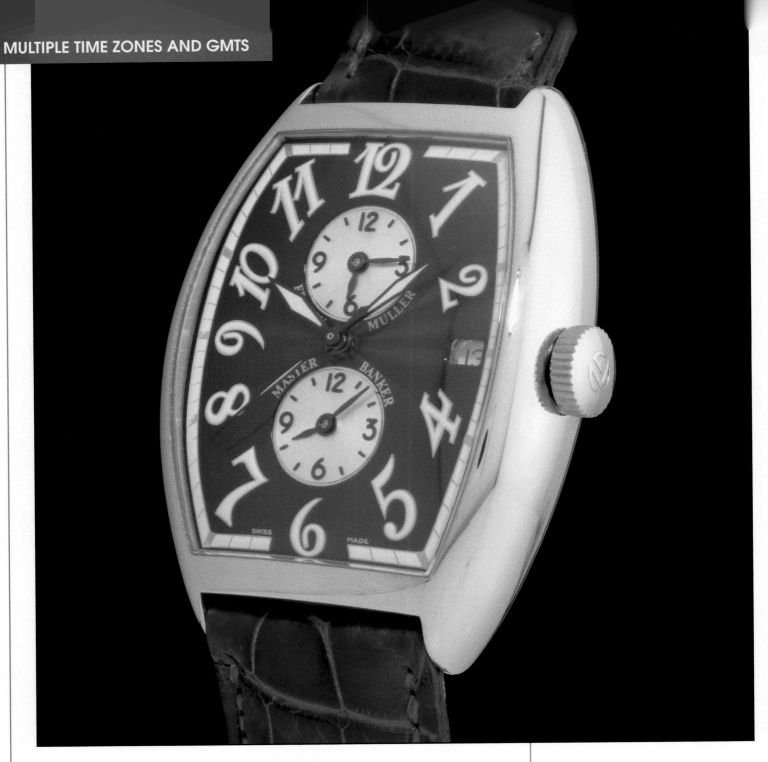

FRANCK MULLER - CINTREE CURVEX MASTER BANKER

This self-winding Franck Muller modified caliber 2800 is a triple time-zone movement, shows a particular arrangement of the time-related indications and fits well to all the dial shapes adopted by the brand. All adjustments, including date correction, are performed via a single crown. The case is realized in three different sizes and the dial is white or blue.

FRANCK MULLER - LONG ISLAND MASTER BANKER

The architecture of the Long Island line modernizes the Art Deco spirit, defining its peculiar characters with geometric aspects. The rectangular shape matches the regulator-type arrangement typical for the Master Banker dials, assuring a clear reading of information. With respect to the genuine regulators, the two opposite subdials indicate an additional time on a 12-hour basis with double hands. A single crown sets the time of the three-hand couples.

FRANCK MULLER - TRANSAMERICA GRAND REVEIL GMT

This self-winding Franck Muller caliber 7850 (base Girard-Perregaux caliber 2291) offers dual-time readout. Indications and displays are arranged as those on other models with the same functions. On the round dial, the numerals are exhibited in Franck Muller's typical style with a generous use of color and luminescent material.

FRANCK MULLER - TRANSAMERICA WORLDWIDE

The Transamerica Worldwide houses the self-winding caliber 2800 with dual-time readout and adopts the traditional scheme based on an independent center hand and doubles the time scale on the bezel on a 24-hour basis. The luminous guilloché dial exhibits large black hands with a luminescent layer. The GMT serpentine hand is adjusted by extracting the crown by one click to put the indication forward by a clockwise turn. The digital date display is adjusted via the same crown position, but by turning it counterclockwise. The same crown adjusts the time.

GÉRALD GENTA - ARENA SPORT GMT PERPETUAL CALENDAR

This Arena Sport GMT Perpetual Calendar has a 45mm titanium case with platinum bezel. It is equipped with an automatic movement with perpetual calendar. A 24-hour dial at 12:00 serves as a second time-zone indicator. It offers 45 hours of power reserve.

GIRARD-PERREGAUX - TRAVELLER II

The basic movement adopted for this model has been radically modified by Girard-Perregaux and is supplied also to other houses. Here, the alarm function combined with the dual-time feature is at its best. The model is characterized by a typically sportsmanlike look and is proposed in two case sizes. The additional time zone is displayed at 12:00 (the hours appear once at a time with starlets in the intervals) and the date is at 6:00. The crown at 2:00 winds, sets, and switches the alarm system on and off; the crown positioned at 4:00 adjusts the time of both time zones and corrects the date.

GIRARD-PERREGAUX - VINTAGE 1945 CHRONOGRAPH GMT

Another important Vintage introduction for the brand is the Vintage 1945 Chronograph GMT, King Size. Available in all three colors of gold, the Chronograph GMT houses the automatic mechanical GP 033 CO movement with 61 rubies. The bold square watch features four counters: small seconds at 3:00, hours at 6:00, minutes at 9:00, and a GMT 24-hour indicator at 12:00.

HARRY WINSTON - EXCENTER TIMEZONE

The launch of the first Excenter timepiece by Harry Winston in 2002 ushered in a new generation of complicated watches for the brand. With off-center counters, this Excenter Timezone watch houses the Jacquet 7060 mechanical movement that enables a second time zone to be read off a 24-hour retrograde counter. It offers 5 days of power reserve, displayed at 12:00. The date aperture is at 6:00 and the hours and minutes are on the right side of the dial with a luminous day/night indicator below it. The second time zone is shown on a 24-hour retrograde counter on the left side of the dial. This distinctive watch uses a world-first compensating toothed gear with no backlash to ensure greater precision of the hour and minute display. The dial combines elegance and legibility. The 39mm watch is crafted in 18-karat white gold and is water resistant to 30 meters.

Multiple Time Zones and GMTs

HARRY WINSTON - PREMIER PERPETUAL CALENDAR TIMEZONE

Perpetuating the tradition of the Premier collection, Harry Winston combines the perpetual calendar function with two time zones in this model. The perpetual calendar indicates the date and day on small dials at 3:00 and 9:00 respectively, while the months and leap years are displayed at 12:00. The second time zone appears at 6:00 on a dual-colored day/night 24-hour counter. The GMT function is set using a screw-on pushpiece. The perpetual calendar will function without adjustment until February 28, 2100. The watch, with automatic GP3306 movement, is crafted in an edition of 55 18-karat white-gold pieces and 45 18-karat rose-gold pieces.

IWC - SPITFIRE UTC REF. 3251

IWC's Spitfire UTC is crafted in steel and houses the caliber 37526 automatic movement, which oscillates at 28,800 vibrations per hour and features 21 rubies. It offers date indicator and 24-hour display. The time is adjusted in one-hour intervals and features a center second hand with stop device. The watch houses a soft iron inner case for protection against magnetic fields. It is water resistant to 60 meters.

JAEGER-LECOULTRE - MASTER COMPRESSOR DUALMATIC

The Jaeger-LeCoultre Master Compressor Dualmatic watch is dedicated to the traveler. It offers local and 24-hour time. Elegantly housed in a 41.5mm case, the Dualmatic is fitted with the Caliber 972 high-performance automatic movement. It vibrates at 28,800 vibrations per hour and offers 50 hours of power reserve. The movement is composed of 230 parts and 29 jewels. It offers hours, minutes, small seconds and date at the travel time, hours of reference time, 24-hour indicator synchronized with reference time and a rotating flange to protect against accidental rotation. It is fitted with one crown with compression key at 2:00 to adjust the rotating bezel and one crown with compression key at 4:00 for initial setting and starting, and moving the principal hour marker forwards or backwards. The caseback features an 18-karat gold 1000 Hours Control medallion.

JAEGER-LECOULTRE - MASTER GEOGRAPHIC

Housing the self-winding JLC Caliber 929/3, this dual-time watch is a descendant of the Géographique, the first watch to combine world time and the hours and minutes of a second time zone. The Master Geographic adopts the same movement with a change in the position of the window where the names of the 24 reference towns related to their respective time zones appear (in this version at 6:00). The 24-hour indication of the second time zone may be changed into the day/night display. The new white-gold version is supplied with a sapphire-crystal caseback with a hinged cover.

JAEGER-LECOULTRE - MASTER HOMETIME

This Master Hometime watch houses Jaeger-LeCoultre's new mechanical automatic movement 975 that beats at 28,000 vibrations an hour. It offers 50 hours of power reserve and features 230 parts and 29 jewels. The local hour hand (for travel time) can be moved backwards or forwards, date function is synchronized with the local hour hand, the home- or reference-time hour hand, day/night indicator and minutes and small seconds hand. It is crafted in 18-karat pink gold and in stainless steel and is water resistant to 50 meters.

JAEGER-LECOULTRE - REVERSO DUOFACE

This model's manual-winding JLC Caliber 854 offers dual time zone readout with additional dial. Through a rather complex caliber modification it was possible to obtain the time indication of two time zones on the two opposite dials typical for the Reverso models by using the same movement (created in 1994, consisting of 180 components). On the first dial is a classic design of hours, minutes and small seconds of the home time; on the second dial (the rear case side), the time of the additional time zone is shown on a 24-hour basis in a slightly off-center position at 6:00. To adjust the latter display it is necessary to actuate a corrector placed on the case middle.

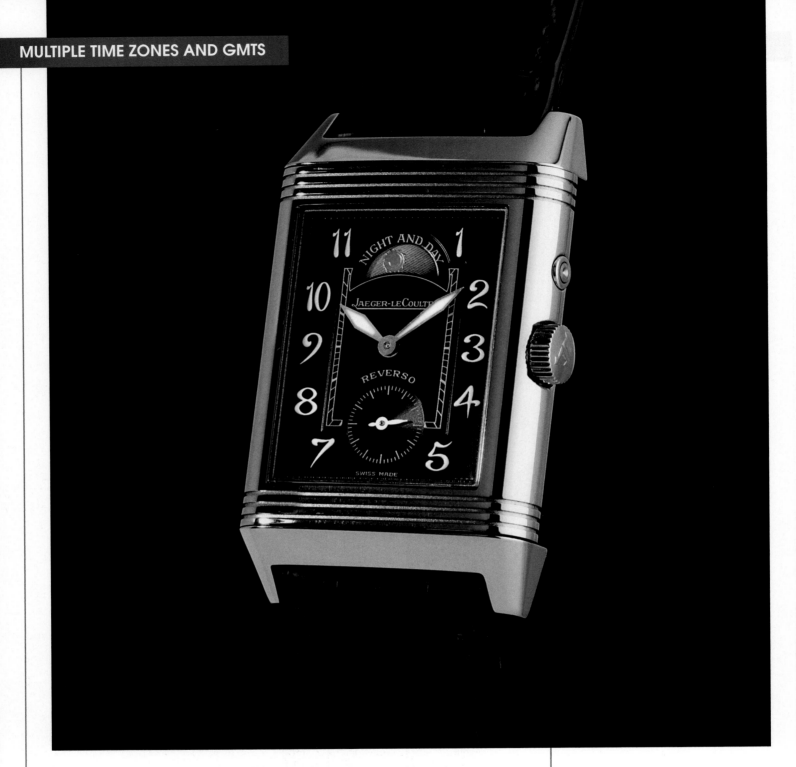

JAEGER-LECOULTRE - REVERSO DUOFACE NIGHT/DAY

The manual-winding JLC Caliber 854J offers dual time with a day/night indicator. A modification of the 854 caliber resulted in this new edition of the Reverso Duoface whose unusual design of the main dial exhibits the day/night indication in a window placed at 12:00. Luminescent hands and enameled markers are combined, according to the brand's new esthetic choices, with a black-enameled dial and stylized Chinese numerals in the Reverso models supplied with white-gold cases.

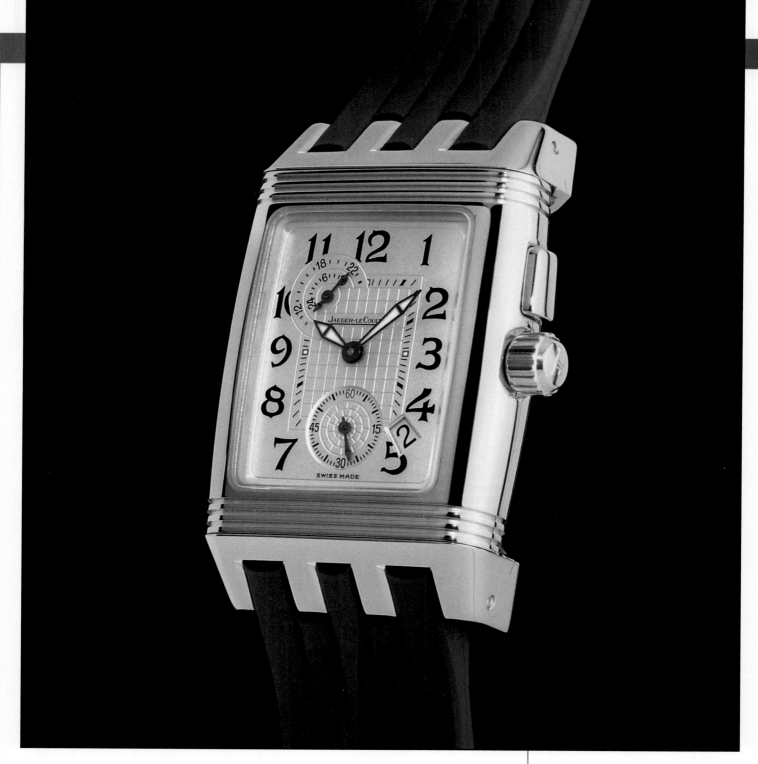

JAEGER-LECOULTRE - REVERSO GRAN'SPORT DUOFACE

The Gran'Sport Duoface houses the JLC Caliber 851, in which a single movement is able to coordinate the workings of seven hands: on the first dial, the main time is shown via the unusual indication by a single hand on a 24-hour basis on circle sectors. The opposite dial is dedicated totally to the second time zone, displayed on a 24-hour day/night basis in a more traditional way. Fast correction of the second time zone is carried out by means of a pusher (each pressure corresponds to a one-hour step forward).

JAEGER-LECOULTRE - REVERSO GRAN'SPORT LADY

The display of dual time zones on opposite dials, both combined for the first time with a day/night indication, is the main feature of the Gran'Sport Duoface Lady. Housing the JLC Caliber 864, the time exhibited on the second face (enriched by two rows of 16 diamonds) is adjusted independently by a corrector positioned at 2:00.

JAEGER-LECOULTRE - REVERSO GRANDE GMT

The principle of two watches in one—such as the Reverso—has long delighted watch connoisseurs. The Reverso Grande GMT features a single movement driving back-to-back dials displaying different time zones. Crafted in steel or in pink gold, the front dial displays hours, minutes, large date, small seconds, and day/night indicator. The dial has a silvered guilloché wave design. The contrasting black back dial features the 8-day power-reserve indicator and the symmetrically arranged day/night indicator, as well as the extraordinary GMT device. The watch is powered by the manually wound Caliber 878 that beats at 28,800 vibrations per hour, consisting of 276 parts and 35 jewels.

JAQUET DROZ - LES DOUZE VILLES EMAIL

Created in a limited edition of 88 pieces, this jumping hour and 12 time-zone watch houses the Jaquet Droz caliber 3663-4 self-winding mechanical movement with double barrels. The jumping hours are visible through an aperture at 12:00 and the 12 time zones are depicted through an aperture that displays 12 international cities' names. The 18-karat white-gold watch houses 28 jewels, offers 72 hours of power reserve, and is water resistant to 30 meters.

PATEK PHILIPPE - WORLD TIME

This model, housing the caliber 240/188 with the Geneva Seal, is inspired by the Patek World Time watches of the 1930s. It is the result of four years spent developing a patented mechanism that allows simultaneous corrections of local time, reference town and 24 hour (by one-hour increments) by a singles pusher. A clutch-like system allows selecting and changing the time zone without influencing the movement's running. In fact, the hour hand is independent from the minute hand that continues turning even during corrections. Once the reference town relevant to a time zone is set at 12 and the corresponding time by the crown, the world-time function runs automatically and at every push of the button all the indications advance by one time zone.

ROGER DUBUIS - COLLECTION GOLDENSQUARE,
GRANDE COMPLICATION REF. G43 5729 0 5.7A

From the famed GoldenSquare series by Roger Dubuis, this watch is crafted in 18-karat polished and satin-finished white gold. The 43mm case is water resistant to 3atm and houses the mechanical self-wind RD5729 caliber with 25 jewels and decorated with the Côtes de Genève pattern. It is adjusted in five positions and marked with the Geneva Quality Hallmark. The watch offers instantaneous perpetual calendar with five apertures and dual time zones. The perpetual calendar indicates days of week, large date and months at 12:00, leap year at 4:00, dual time zones with moonphase at 6:00, and day/night indicator at 8:00. Only 28 pieces are being created.

ULYSSE NARDIN - SONATA

An unusual but useful marriage between second time zone and alarm is an "haute de gamme" proposal from the manufacture of Le Locle. An impressive 41mm case houses the twin-barrel UN 66 caliber, created by scientist and master watchmaker Dr. Ludwig Oechslin. As for the usual features of this manufacture, the main time for travelers can be set quickly using the two pushers integrated into the middle design, while the home hour is located in the subdial located at 6:00 on a 24-hour scale. The alarm function is one of the most sophisticated ever seen: hour and minute are set on a subdial, while the countdown indicator shows the remaining time on the ring. Alarm on-off is shown at 9:00 and at 7:30 a small circular window is open on the ring-speed regulator, as for the minute repeaters.

Multiple Time Zones and GMTs

ZENITH - DUAL TIME

This self-winding chronometer (Zenith caliber Elite 682) offers dual time readout. The basic 661 caliber has been modified in order to obtain various configurations: an arrow-tip center hand adjustable by the pusher positioned at 10:00, a small second subdial at 9:00, and a digital date display. The waterproof case demonstrates a classic linear style. The silvered dial is decorated with an eggshell pattern and the hour ring is grained.

ZENITH - GRANDE CLASS ELITE DUAL TIME

The Grande Class Elite Dual Time watch allows the wearer to read off the time in Paris and New York simultaneously. Time is adjusted easily by a pushpiece at 10:00. This new Elite 683 automatic extra-flat caliber is housed in a steel or yellow-, white- or pink-gold case, holds 36 jewels and beats at 28,800 vibrations per hour.

NOVELTIES

A wealth of complex watches that exist on the market

fall into their own categories warranting

attention. Though less complicated

than the haute horlogerie

functions, those such as

astronomical indicators,

regulators and alarms,

and others offer

functions desired by

today's collectors.

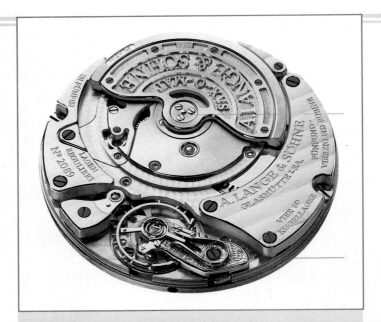

Regulators have a long history. They were extremely accurate clocks used to compare and calibrate the rate of standard timepieces.

While di Dondi's was the first known astronomical clock (created in the mid 1300s), it was not until the 15th and 16th centuries that clockmakers began creating clocks with moonphases and other scenes from above on them. Astronomical indicators are one of the most telling aspects of man's ongoing fascination with the sun, moon and stars.

Regulators also have a long history. Originally, they were extremely accurate clocks used to compare and calibrate the rate of standard timepieces. Eventually, the regulator evolved into a configuration for use to determine longitude at sea. From there, it evolved into the pocket watch's designs and has since become a coveted aesthetic for wristwatches, much desired for its off-centered appeal.

All types of alarms are available, including those that buzz and those that chime or play tunes. An alarm by any sound, however, is the same: a watch that can be set, often in two zones, to remind its wearer that it's time to do something important.

A host of other novelties such as those with traveling-time readouts, hand-enameled dials and the like are also complex novelties worthy of our attention.

A. LANGE & SÖHNE - LANGEMATIK

The Langematik is the first self-winding wristwatch with the zero-reset mechanism and a patented world-first time-setting device that instantly sets the seconds' hand to zero when the crown is pulled. It houses the L921.4 Sax-O-Mat movement with outsized date and features a bi-directional winding three-quarter rotor made of gold with a platinum mass.

CHOPARD - L.U.C 4R QUATTRO REGULATEUR

From its L.U.C collection, Chopard releases the 4R Quattro Regulateur. Crafted in 18-karat rose or white gold, the watch houses the L.U.C mechanical hand-wound movement with 224 parts and 39 jewels. Offering 9 days of power reserve, the COSC-certified chronometer has time-zone indicator and semi-instantaneous date display.

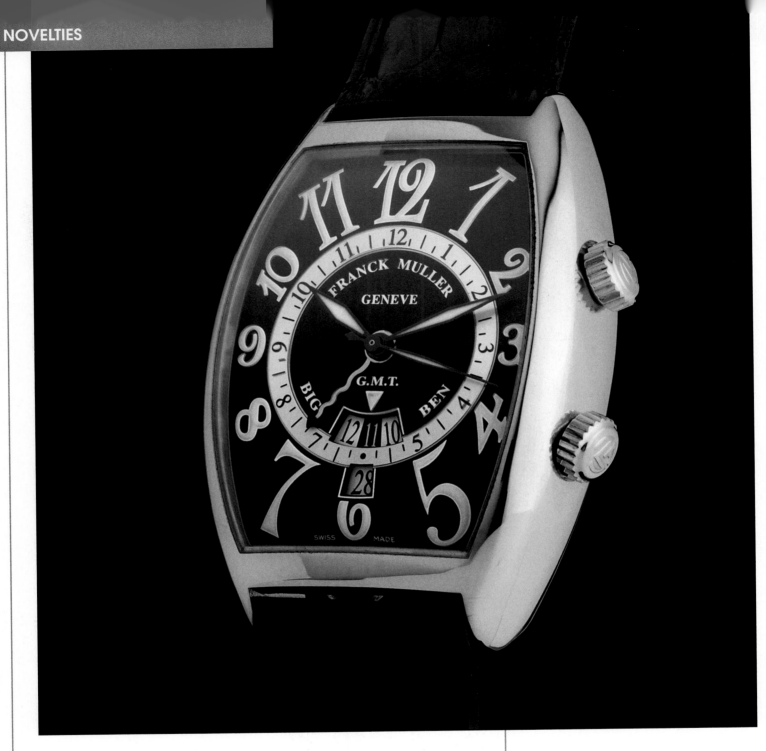

FRANCK MULLER – CINTREE CURVEX BIG BEN GMT

This watch houses the self-winding movement, Franck Muller caliber FM 7850, with hour, minute, second, date, and second time zone. The Big Ben GMT is extra large (41.7x35mm) and features a GMT and alarm function and two independent crowns. The crown at 2:00 sets the strike-work. When pulled out, it frees the movement and activates the alarm system at the passage of the serpentine hand on the set hour. The crown at 4:00 winds the movement and sets the home time and that of the second time zone.

FRANCK MULLER - TRANSAMERICA GRAND RÉVEIL GMT

Housing the self-winding Franck Muller caliber FM 7850 on a Girard-Perregaux base, this Transamerica Grand Réveil GMT offers hour, minute, second, date, second time zone and alarm. Strike-work (winding and alarm setting) is controlled by the crown at 2:00; time setting of the main hands, the second time zone and date correction are performed via the crown at 4:00.

GIRARD-PERREGAUX - OPERA THREE REF. 99790

The Opera Three is an extremely refined musical watch capable of indicating the passing of time with a melody at each hour. The heart of this watch is a miniature carillon with 20 keys and one drum set with 150 hand-assembled pins. It is possible to choose from two melodies by changing the position of the drum with a small lever. Another lever with three positions allows the wearer to deactivate the melody, to make it play at will or to activate the melody at each hour. The dial has a small seconds subdial at 6:00 and two indicators at 2:00 and 10:00: the power reserve of the carillon and the selected melody, respectively.

GIRARD-PERREGAUX - SEA HAWK II

The Sea Hawk was claimed in 1959 for the Girard-Perregaux's diving watches and in the 1970s the watches were first provided with a screw-down crown and turning ring. Now the Sea Hawk II appears with a titanium or steel case in two sizes (40 or 42mm). A protected screw-down crown, a turning ring in gold with an embossed scale and an antireflective sapphire crystal are the outstanding features of this model. The 50-hour power-reserve indicator appears on an opaline black dial with luminescent numerals or on a matte black dial with ruthenium-gray or sapphire-blue applied numerals. The watch is water resistant to 30 meters.

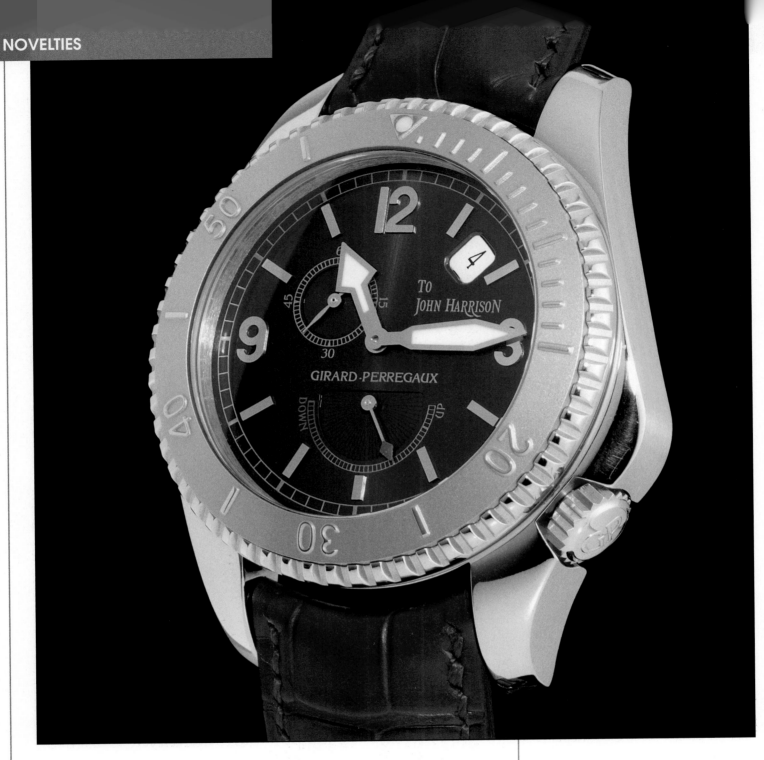

GIRARD-PERREGAUX - SEA HAWK II JOHN HARRISON

This special version with a 42mm case is dedicated to John Harrison, an English watchmaker, who invented marine chronometers, i.e. extremely precise watches capable of calculating the longitude when on board. The technical features of the Sea Hawk II are combined with different case materials (gray, yellow and pink gold or stainless steel with a gray-gold ring) and a dial with the small second subdial at 10:00.

GIRARD-PERREGAUX - TRAVELLER II

This self-winding Caliber 2291 Traveller II watch offers hour, minute, second, date, second time zone and two independent winding crowns. The movement adopted for this model is modified by Girard-Perregaux for the dual time function. The crown at 2:00 winds the watch, one counterclockwise click sets the second zone's time and one clockwise click corrects the date (this position also activates the strike-work). The crown positioned at 4:00 winds the alarm system (closed position) and sets the main time (first click).

HARRY WINSTON - OPUS 4

The fourth in Harry Winston's ingenious Opus series of timepieces developed in conjunction with independent watchmakers, the Opus 4 is a true grand complication. Created with Christophe Claret, the master of chiming watches, the Opus 4 is a completely reversible minute-repeater striking on cathedral gongs. One face of the watch reveals the tourbillon and the other features a large moonphase indication with date. The movement, which reverses the direction of the hands for each face, is housed in a platinum Premier case signed by Harry Winston. It is comprised of 423 parts, including 40 jewels, and has 53 hours of power reserve. The Ø 44mm case is water resistant to 30 meters and features a mechanism that allows its reversal. Only 18 platinum Opus 4 models and two high-jeweled versions will be created.

IWC - AQUATIMER MINUTE MEMORY

IWC created an horological and technical marvel in this watch: it is the first diver's watch to be equipped with a separately operated minute-memory mechanism. Divers working with IWC indicated that the ability to measure a second intermediate time independently (such as the duration of a diver's ascent) would be an extremely sensible and practical improvement. Essentially, in addition to the chronograph function, this watch offers another flyback minute hand that can be activated under water at any point in the operating depth range, and which can also serve an emergency backup system if the decompression computer fails. The Aquatimer Minute Memory watch is offered exclusively in titanium and is pressure and water resistant to 2,000 meters. IWC has filed for several patents for this professional instrument.

JAEGER-LECOULTRE - GYROTOURBILLON I

Jaeger-LeCoultre's new patented GyroTourbillon I houses the complex 512-part Caliber 177 complete with a built-in running equation-of-time mechanism, as well as a host of other functions and indications. The exquisite escapement is a first in the history of the tourbillon with respect to its spherical design, whose multi-dimensional rotation is fascinating, as well as technical advancements. In addition to depicting the hours and minutes, the dial also indicates the remaining power reserve, date, month and true solar time as part of the equation-of-time function. The perpetual calendar won't require manual intervention until February 28, 2100. The spherical tourbillon features an aluminum case and an inner titanium and aluminum carriage that is positioned at a 90-degree angle to the outer case, and rotates 2.5 times faster than its companion. The total weight of this spherical wonder is just 0.33 grams.

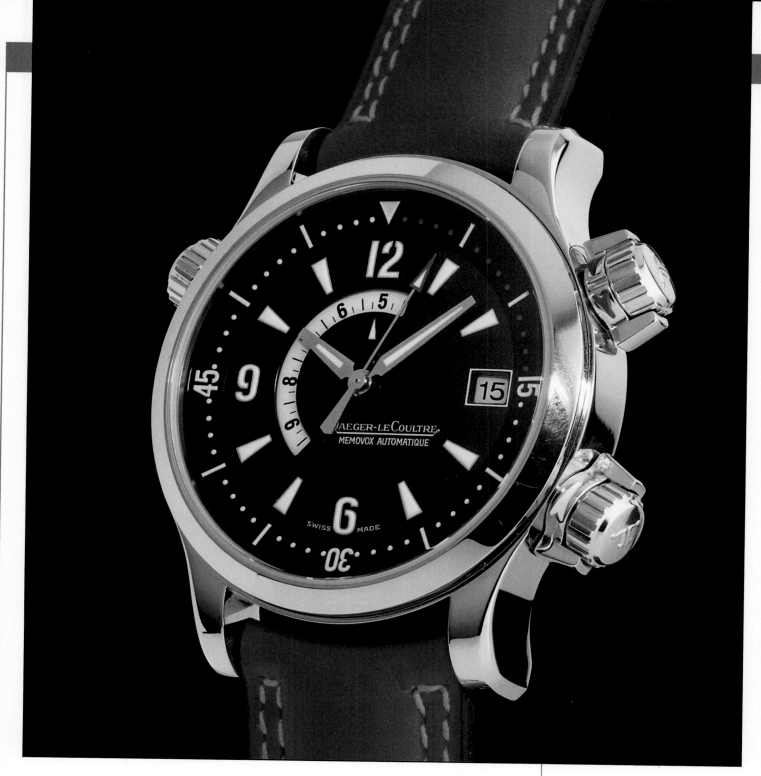

JAEGER-LECOULTRE - MASTER COMPRESSOR MEMOVOX

Housing the JLC caliber 918, this self-winding watch offers hour, minute, second and date. An unusual patented protection system of the two crowns placed on the right case side allows the Master Compressor to be water resistant up to 10atm, a very high standard for an alarm watch. This so-called "pressure" solution is based on a turning element (a kind of key) with two positions (closed and open): in the closed position the crown is locked by gasket compression, in the opened it is unlocked and ready for activation. In this way, high water resistance and duration standards are assured by far better results than those offered by the "screw" solution. This system was not necessary for the third crown, placed at 10:00.

JAEGER-LECOULTRE - MASTER REVEIL

The automatic-winding 918 caliber produced by Jaeger-LeCoultre and housed in this watch is provided with a rotor with a 21-karat gold sector. The power reserve assures autonomy of 45 hours. Separate systems are used for winding and time-setting operations by a crown at 2:00 for the alarm system and another at 4:00 for the movement. This watch was tested over 1,000 hours and the case is water resistant up to 5atm. The dial with a center turning disc features a luminescent alarm-set pointer.

Grand Complications

JAQUET DROZ - GRANDE SECONDE MARINE

With an elegant regulator dial, this COSC-certified marine chronometer houses the Jaquet Droz 2663-4 self-winding mechanical movement that beats at 28,800 vibrations per hour. It features a 22-karat white-gold oscillating weight, 30 jewels, and 72 hours of power reserve. It is water resistant to 100 meters.

PATEK PHILIPPE - GONDOLO CALENDARIO

The Annual Calendar Ref. 5135 is officially referred to as the Gondolo Calendario and offers a patented annual calendar function and moonphase. The proprietary caliber was developed in 1996 and was the first wristwatch to automatically advance the month, day and date with only one manual correction on March 1. The caliber 324 self-winding mechanical movement features the Gyromax balance wheel (for which Patek Philippe garnered patents more than 50 years ago) and an entirely new toothing system. The new teeth assure constant force transmission, positively impacting the watch's rate of accuracy. The caliber 324 meets the specifications of the Geneva Seal and is revealed through a sapphire caseback.

PATEK PHILIPPE - SKY MOON REF. 5102

The incredible Celestial Ref. 5102 Sky Moon wristwatch is based on the achievements of two watch predecessors (including the Star Caliber). The dial of this astronomical wonder depicts the exact configuration of the night sky, complete with the stars' movements, the position of the moon and its phases within the lunar cycle. Two years in the making, the celestial watch houses a complex astronomical self-winding mechanical movement comprised of 301 components, including 45 jewels. To replicate the movement of the heavenly bodies on the surface of the dial, Patek Philippe developed a highly sophisticated system of layered discs, each of which turns at a different speed to create the necessary precision, while at the same time offering a sense of depth and reality.

PARMIGIANI FLEURIER - BUGATTI TYPE 370

An innovative new timepiece is the Bugatti type 370, powered by the Parmigiani Fleurier 370 caliber. This model took Michel Parmigiani and a team of experts three years to perfect and it is the first wristwatch to be built totally on a transverse axis. Every detail of the watch is designed with its namesake automobile in mind. The movement wheels are designed to reflect the aesthetic appearance of the wheel rim invented by Ettore Bugatti in the 1930s and the two dedicated wheels in the movement feature arms cut according to the same design. Crafted in 18-karat white gold, its eight-part case makes observing the movement very easy with its six sapphire crystals, cambered and domed to the extreme. Only 50 pieces will be made per year for the next three years.

VACHERON CONSTANTIN - TRIBUTE TO THE GREAT EXPLORERS

The 18-karat gold Tribute to the Great Explorers watches are powered by a patented mechanism that provides an original display of hours and minutes. The design of the Tribute to the Great Explorers line incorporates the brand's famous Maltese Cross logo into the movement and, building on the Vacheron Constantin self-winding caliber 1126AT, this watch houses a series of original devices. The time display is always moving, traveling over the land and sea that have been hand-painted on the two-disc dial. Each version's main dial depicts the area associated with the honored explorer's travels. The second, lower dial forms the bottom arc of the watch face and bears the minute track. Each watch is delivered in a solid wood presentation case, complete with magnifying glass to view the delicate enamel work. The first watches pay tribute to Ferdinand Magellan and Zheng He.

GLOSSARY

ACCURACY s. Precision

ALARM WATCH (image 1 - 2)
A watch provided with a movement capable of releasing an acoustic sound at the time set. A second crown is dedicated to the winding, setting and release of the striking-work; an additional center hand indicates the time set. The section of the movement dedicated to the alarm device is made up by a series of wheels linked with the barrel, an escapement and a hammer (s.) striking a gong (s.) or bell (s.). Works much like a normal alarm clock.

AMPLITUDE
Maximum angle by which a balance or pendulum wings from its rest position.

ANALOG or **ANALOGUE**
A watch displaying time indications by means of hands.

ANTIMAGNETIC
Said of a watch whose movement is not influenced by electromagnetic fields that could cause two or more windings of the balance-spring to stick to each other, consequently accelerating the rate of the watch. This effect is obtained by adopting metal alloys (e.g. Nivarox) resisting magnetization.

ANTIREFLECTION, ANTIREFLECTIVE
Superficial glass treatment assuring the dispersion of reflected light. Better results are obtained if both sides are treated, but in order to avoid scratches on the upper layer, the treatment of the inner surface is preferred.

ARBOR
Bearing element of a gear (s.) or balance, whose ends—called pivots (s.)—run in jewel (s.) holes or brass bushings.

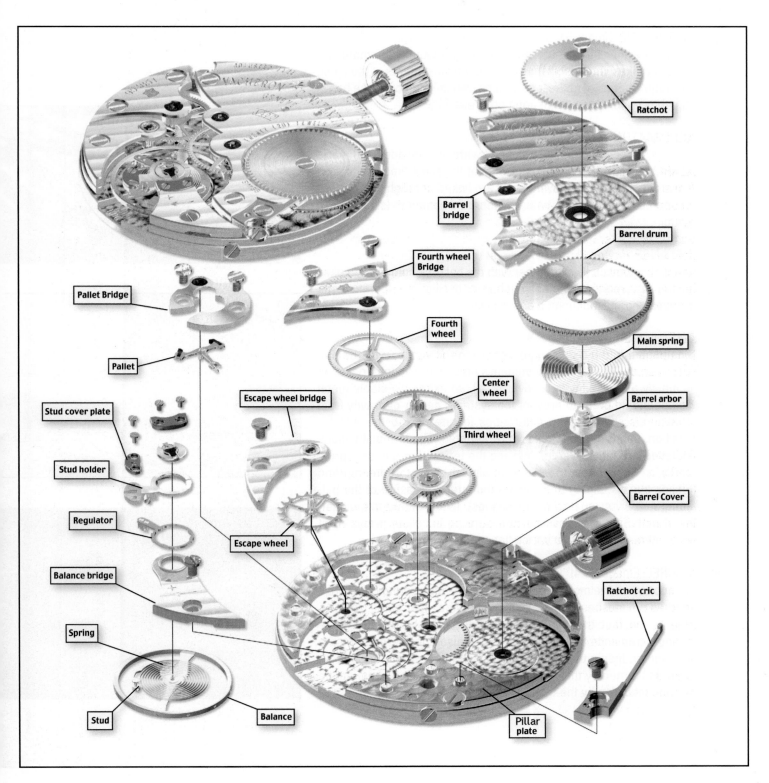

Ratchot

Barrel bridge

Barrel drum

Fourth wheel Bridge

Main spring

Pallet Bridge

Fourth wheel

Barrel arbor

Pallet

Center wheel

Stud cover plate

Escape wheel bridge

Third wheel

Barrel Cover

Stud holder

Regulator

Balance bridge

Escape wheel

Ratchot cric

Spring

Stud

Balance

Pillar plate

AUTOMATIC (image 1)

A watch whose mechanical movement (s.) is wound automatically. A rotor makes short oscillations due to the movements of the wrist. Through a series of gears, oscillations transmit motion to the barrel (s.), thus winding the mainspring progressively.

AUTOMATON

Figures, placed on the dial or case of watches, provided with parts of the body or other elements moving at the same time as the sonnerie (s.) strikes. The moving parts are linked, through an aperture on the dial or caseback, with the sonnerie hammers (s.) striking a gong.

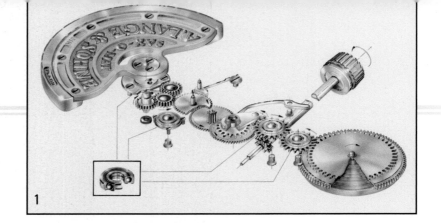

BALANCE (image 2)

Oscillating device that, together with the balance spring (s.), makes up the movement's heart inasmuch as its oscillations determine the frequency of its functioning and precision.

BALANCE SPRING (image 2)

Component of the regulating organ (s.) that, together with the balance (s.), determines the movement's precision. The material used is mostly a steel alloy (e.g. Nivarox, s.), an extremely stable metal compound. In order to prevent the system's center of gravity from continuous shifts, hence differences in rate due to the watch's position, some modifications were adopted. These modifications included Breguet's overcoil (closing the terminal part of the spring partly on itself, so as to assure an almost perfect centering) and Philips curve (helping to eliminate the lateral pressure of the balance-staff pivots against their bearings). Today, thanks to the quality of materials, it is possible to assure an excellent precision of movement working even with a flat spring.

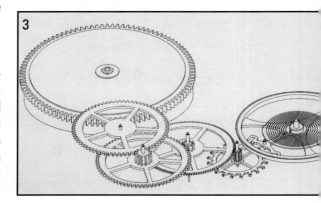

BARREL (image 3 - 4)

Component of the movement containing the mainspring (s.), whose toothed rim meshes with the pinion of the first gear of the train (s.). Due to the fact that the whole—made up of barrel and mainspring—transmits the motive force, it is also considered to be the very motor. Inside the barrel, the mainspring is wound around an arbor (s.) turned by the winding crown or, in the case of automatic movements, also by the gear powered by the rotor (s.).

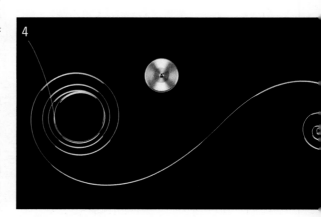

1

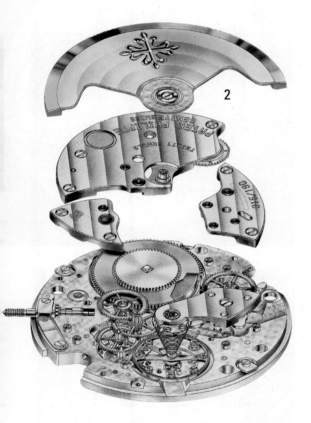

2

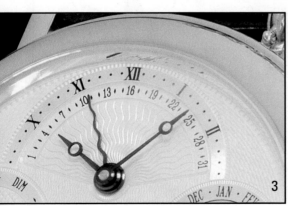

3

BEARING
Part on which a pivot turns, in watches mostly a jewels (s.).

BEVELING (image 1)
Chamfering of edges of levers, bridges and other elements of a movement by 45∞, a treatment typically found in high-grade movements.

BEZEL
Top part of case (s.), sometimes holds the crystal. It may be integrated with the case middle (s.) or a separate element. It is snapped or screwed on to the middle.

BOTTOM PLATE s. Pillar-plate

BRACELET
A metal band attached to the case. It is called integral if there is no apparent discontinuity between case and bracelet and the profile of attachments is similar to the first link.

BRIDGE (image 2)
Structural metal element of a movement (s.)—sometimes called cock or bar—supporting the wheel train (s.), balance (s.), escapement (s.) and barrel (s.). Each bridge is fastened to the plate (s.) by means of screws and locked in a specific position by pins. In high-quality movements the sight surface is finished with various types of decoration.

BREGUET HANDS (image 3)
A particular type of hands in a traditional elegant shape.

BRUSHED, BRUSHING
Topical finishing giving metals a line finish, a clean and uniform look.

CABOCHON (image 4)
Any kind of precious stone, such as sapphire, ruby or emerald, uncut and only polished, generally of a half-spherical shape, mainly used as an ornament of the winding crown (s.) or certain elements of the case.

CALENDAR, ANNUAL

An intermediate complication between a simple calendar and a perpetual calendar. This feature displays all the months with 30 or 31 days correctly, but needs a manual correction at the end of February. Generally, date, day of the week and month, or only day and month are displayed on the dial.

CALENDAR, GREGORIAN

With respect to the Julian Calendar (s. Calendar, Julian), the calendar reform introduced by Pope Gregory XIII in 1582 corrected the slight error of the former calendar by suppressing a leap year every hundred years, except for years whose numbers are divisible by 400 (this entailed the elimination of the leap years in 1700, 1800 and 1900, but not in 2000 and 2400). In non-Catholic countries this reform was introduced after 1700.

CALENDAR, FULL

Displaying date, day of the week and month on the dial, but needing a manual correction at the end of a month with less than 31 days. It is often combined with the moonphase (s).

CALENDAR, JULIAN

The calendar established by Julius Caesar was based on the year duration of 365.25 days with a leap year with 366 days every 4 years. In 325 AD, this calendar was adopted by the Church. Due to the slight error (0.0078 day) implied in this time count, the Julian Calendar was later replaced by the Gregorian Calendar (s. Calendar, Gregorian).

CALENDAR, PERPETUAL (image 1)

This is the most complex horology complication related to the calendar feature, as it indicates the date, day, month and leap year and does not need manual corrections until the year 2100 (when the leap year will be ignored).

CALIBER (image 2)

Originally it indicated only the size (in lines, "') of a movement (s.), but now this indication defines a specific movement type and combines it with the constructor's name and identification number. Therefore the caliber identifies the movement.

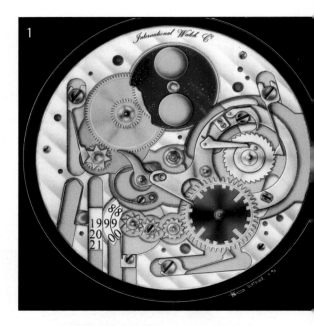

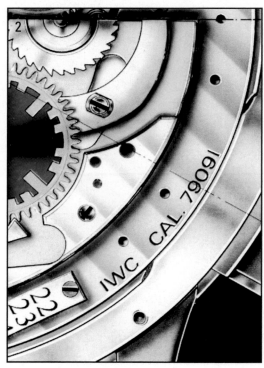

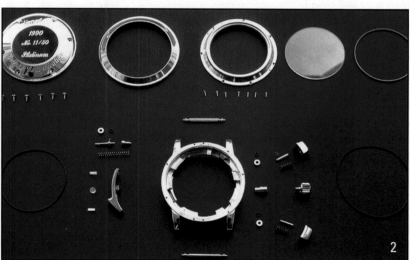

CANNON
An element in the shape of a hollow cylinder, sometimes also called pipe or bush, for instance the pipe of the hour wheel bearing the hour hand.

CHAPTER-RING
Hour-circle, i.e. the hour numerals arranged on a dial.

CAROUSEL
Device similar to the tourbillon (s.), but with the carriage not driven by the fourth wheel, but by the third wheel.

CARRIAGE or TOURBILLON CARRIAGE (image 1)
Rotating frame of a tourbillon (s.) device, carrying the balance and escapement (s.). This structural element is essential for a perfect balance of the whole system and its stability, in spite of its reduced weight. As today's tourbillon carriages make a rotation per minute, errors of rate in the vertical position are eliminated. Because of the widespread use of transparent dials, carriages became elements of aesthetic attractiveness.

CASE (image 2)
Container housing and protecting the movement (s.), usually made up of three parts: middle, bezel, and back.

CENTER SECOND HAND, s. Sweep second hand.

CENTER-WHEEL
The minute wheel in a going-train.

CHAMPLEVÉ (image 3)
Hand-made treatment of the dial or case surface. The pattern is obtained by hollowing a metal sheet with a graver and subsequently filling the hollows with enamel.

CHIME
Striking-work equipped with a set of bells that may be capable of playing a complete melody. A watch provided with such a feature is called chiming watch.

CHRONOGRAPH (image 1)
A watch that includes a built-in stopwatch function, i.e. a timer that can be started and stopped to time an event. There are many variations of the chronograph.

CHRONOMETER
A high-precision watch. According to the Swiss law, a manufacture may put the word "chronometer" on a model only after each individual piece has passed a series of tests and obtained a running bulletin and a chronometer certificate by an acknowledged Swiss control authority, such as the COSC (s.).

CIRCULAR GRAINING (image 2)
Superficial decoration applied to bridges, rotors and pillar-plates in the shape of numerous slightly superposed small grains, obtained by using a plain cutter and abrasives. Also called Pearlage or Pearling.

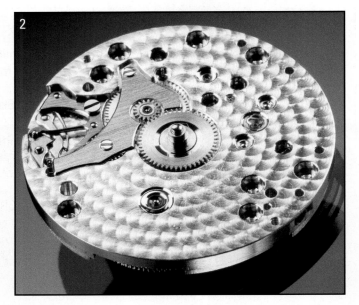

CLICK s. Pawl

CLOISONNÉ (image 3)
A kind of enamel work— mainly used for the decoration of dials—in which the outlines of the drawing are formed by thin metal wires. The colored enamel fills the hollows formed in this way. After oven firing, the surface is smoothed until the gold threads appear again.

CLOUS DE PARIS (image 4)
Decoration of metal parts characterized by numerous small pyramids.

COCK, s. Bridge.

COLIMAÇONNAGE (image 5), s. Snailing.

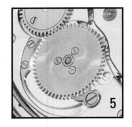

COLUMN-WHEEL (image 1)
Part of chronograph movements, governing the functions of various levers and parts of the chronograph operation, in the shape of a small-toothed steel cylinder. It is controlled by pushers through levers that hold and release it. It is a very precise and usually preferred type of chronograph operation.

COMPLICATION
Additional function with respect to the manual-winding basic movement for the display of hours, minutes and seconds. Today, certain features, such as automatic winding or date, are taken for granted, although they should be defined as complications. The main complications are moonphase (s.), power reserve (s.), GMT (s.), and full calendar (s.). Further functions are performed by the so-called great complications, such as split-second (s.) chronograph, perpetual calendar (s.), tourbilon (s.) device, and minute repeater (s.).

CORRECTOR
Pusher (s.) positioned on the case side that is normally actuated by a special tool for the quick setting of different indications, such as date, GMT (s.), full or perpetual calendar (s.).

COSC
Abbreviation of "Contrôle Officiel Suisse des Chronomètres," the most important Swiss institution responsible for the functioning and precision tests of movements of chronometers (s.). Tests are performed on each individual watch at different temperatures and in different positions before a functioning bulletin and a chronometer certificate are issued, for which a maximum gap of -4/+4 seconds per day is tolerated.

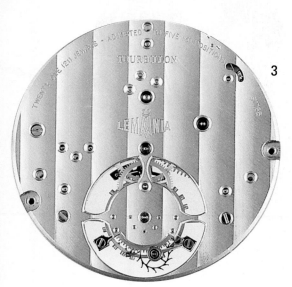

CÔTES CIRCULAIRES (image 2)
Decoration of rotors and bridges of movements, whose pattern consists of a series of concentric ribs.

CÔTES DE GENÈVE (image 3)
Decoration applied mainly to high-quality movements, appearing as a series of parallel ribs, realized by repeated cuts of a cutter leaving thin stripes.

COUNTER (image 1)
Additional hand on a chronograph (s.), indicating the time elapsed since the beginning of the measuring. On modern watches the second counter is placed at the center, while minute and hour counters have off-center hands in special zones (s.), also called subdials.

CROWN
Usually positioned on the case middle (s.) and allows winding, hand setting and often date or GMT hand setting. As it is linked to the movement through the winding stem (s.) passing through a hole in the case. For waterproofing purposes, simple gaskets are used in water-resistant watches, while diving watches adopt screwing systems (screw-down crowns).

CROWN-WHEEL
Wheel meshing with the winding pinion and with the ratchet wheel on the barrel-arbor.

DECK WATCH
A large-sized ship's chronometer.

DEVIATION
A progressive natural change of a watch's rate with respect to objective time. In case of a watch's faster rate, the deviation is defined positive, in the opposite case negative.

DIAL (image 2)
Face of a watch, on which time and further functions are displayed by markers (s.), hands (s.), discs or through windows (s.). Normally it is made of a brass—sometimes silver or gold.

DIGITAL
Said of watches whose indications are displayed mostly inside an aperture or window (s.) on the dial.

EBAUCHE (image 3)
Incomplete (jeweled or non-jeweled) watch movement without regulating organs, mainspring, dial and hands.

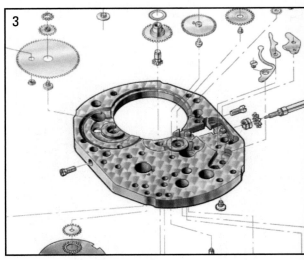

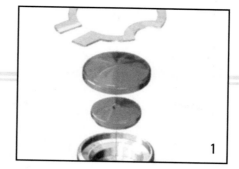

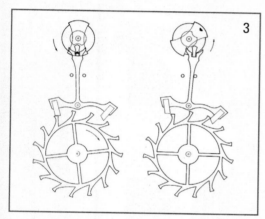

ENDSTONE (image 1)
Undrilled jewel, placed on the balance jewel with the tip of the balance-staff pivot resting against its flat surface, to reduce pivot friction. Sometimes used also for pallet staffs and escape wheels.

ENGINE-TURNED, s. Guilloché.

EQUINOX (image 2)
The time when day and night are of equal length, when the sun is on the plane of the equator. Such times occur twice in a year: the vernal equinox on March 21st-22nd and the autumnal equinox on September 22nd-23rd.

EQUATION OF TIME (image 2)
Indication of the difference, expressed in minutes, between conventional mean time and real solar time. This difference varies from -16 to +16 seconds between one day and the other.

ESCAPE WHEEL (image 3)
A wheel belonging to the mechanism called escapement (s.).

ESCAPEMENT (image 3)
Positioned between the train (s.) and the balance wheel and governing the rotation speed of the wheel-train wheels. In today's horology the most widespread escapement type is the lever escapement. In the past, numerous types of escapements were realized, such as: verge, cylinder, pin-pallet, detent and duplex escapements. Recently, George Daniels developed a so-called "coaxial" escapement.

FLINQUÉ (image 4)
Engraving on the dial or case of a watch, covered with an enamel layer.

FLUTED (image 5)
Said of surfaces worked with thin parallel grooves, mostly on dials or case bezels.

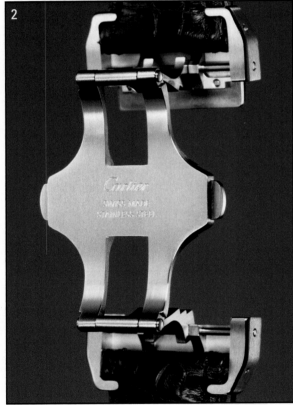

FLY-BACK (image 1)
Feature combined with chronograph (s.) functions, that allows a new measurement starting from zero (and interrupting a measuring already under way) by pressing down a single pusher, i.e. without stopping, zeroing and restarting the whole mechanism. Originally, this function was developed to meet the needs of air forces.

FOLD-OVER CLASP (image 2)
Hinged and jointed element, normally of the same material as the one used for the case. It allows easy fastening of the bracelet on the wrist. Often provided with a snap-in locking device, sometimes with an additional clip or push-piece.

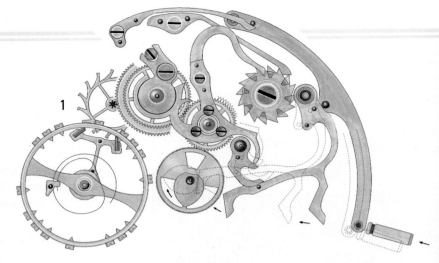

FOURTH-WHEEL
The seconds wheel in a going-train.

FREQUENCY, s. Vibration
Generally defined as the number of cycles per time unit; in horology it is the number of oscillations of a balance every two seconds or of its vibrations per second. For practical purposes, frequency is expressed in vibrations per hour (vph).

FUSEE
A conical part with a spiral groove on which a chain or cord attached to the barrel (s.) is wound. Its purpose is to equalize the driving power transmitted to the train.

GENEVA SEAL (image 3), s. Poinçon de Genève.

GLUCYDUR
Bronze and beryllium alloy used for high-quality balances (s.). This alloy assures high elasticity and hardness values; it is non-magnetic, rustproof and has a very reduced dilatation coefficient, which makes the balance very stable and assures high accuracy of the movement.

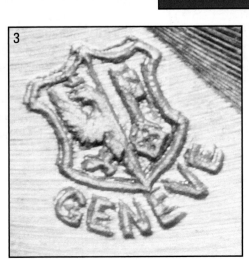

GMT (image 1)
Abbreviation for Greenwich Mean Time. As a feature of watches, it means that two or more time zones are displayed. In this case, the second time may be read from a hand making a full rotation in a 24-hour ring (thereby also indicating whether it is a.m. or p.m. in that zone).

GOING TRAIN s. Train.

GONG (image 2)
Harmonic flattened bell in a steel alloy, generally positioned along the circumference of the movement and struck by hammers (s.) to indicate time by sounds. Size and thickness determine the resulting note and tone. In watches provided with minute-repeaters (s.), there are often two gongs and the hammers strike one note to indicate hours, both notes together to indicate quarters and the other note for the remaining minutes. In more complex models, equipped also with en-passant sonnerie (s.) devices, there may be up to four gongs producing different notes and playing even simple melodies (such as the chime of London's Big Ben).

GRAND (or GREAT) COMPLICATIONS s. Complication

GUILLOCHÉ (image 3)
Decoration of dials, rotors or case parts consisting of patterns made by hand or engine-turned. By the thin pattern of the resulting engravings—consisting of crossing or interlaced lines—it is possible to realize even complex drawings. Dials and rotors decorated in this way are generally in gold or in solid silver.

HAMMER
Steel or brass element used in movements provided with a repeater or alarm sonnerie (s.). It strikes a gong (s.) or bell (s.).

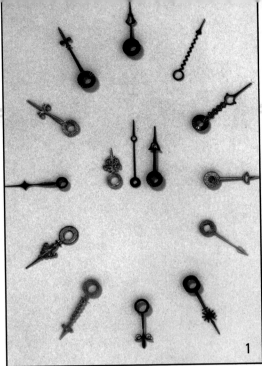

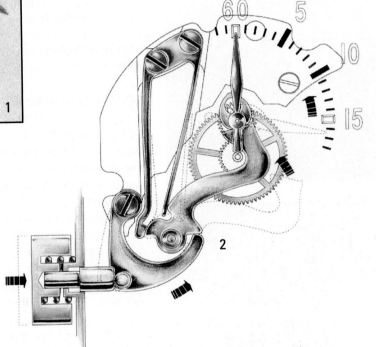

HAND (image 1)
Indicator for the analogue visualization of hours, minutes and seconds as well as other functions. Normally made of brass (rhodium-plated, gilded or treated otherwise), but also steel or gold. Hands are available in different shapes and take part in the aesthetic result of the whole watch.

HEART-PIECE (image 2)
Heart-shaped cam generally used to realign the hands of chronograph counters.

HELIUM VALVE (image 3)
Valve inserted in the case of some professional diving watches to discharge the helium contained in the air mixture inhaled by divers.

HEXALITE
An artificial glass made of a plastic resin.

HUNTER CALIBER
A caliber (s.) characterized by the seconds hand fitted on an axis perpendicular to the one of the winding-stem (s.).

IMPULSE
In a lever escapement (s.) the action of the escape-wheel tooth on the impulse face of the pallet; in the Swiss lever escapement it is produced by the impulse face of the wheel tooth and that of the pallet.

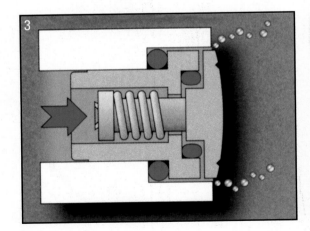

INCABLOC, s. Shockproof.

INDEX s. Regulator

JEWEL (image 1)
Precious stone used in movements as a bearing surface. Generally speaking, the steel pivots (s.) of wheels in movements turn inside synthetic jewels (mostly rubies) lubricated with a drop of oil. The jewel's hardness reduces wear to a minimum even over long periods of time (50 to 100 years). The quality of watches is determined mainly by the shape and finishing of jewels rather than by their number (the most refined jewels have rounded holes and walls to greatly reduce the contact between pivot and stone).

JUMPING HOUR (image 2)
Feature concerning the digital display of time in a window. The indication changes almost instantaneously at every hour.

LEAP-YEAR CYCLE
Leap or bissextile years have 366 days and occur every 4 years (with some exceptions, s. Calendar, Gregorian). Some watches display this datum.

LÉPINE CALIBER
A caliber (s.) typical for pocket-watches, characterized by the seconds hand fitted in the axis of the winding-stem (s.)

LIGNE s. Line.

LINE
Ancient French measuring unit maintained in horology to indicate the diameter of a movement (s.). A line (expressed by the symbol ''') equals 2.255mm. Lines are not divided into decimals; therefore, to indicate measures inferior to the unit, fractions are used (e.g. movements of 13'''3/4 or 10'''1/2).

LUBRICATION

To reduce friction caused by the running of wheels and other parts. There are points to be lubricated with specific low-density oils such as the pivots (s.) turning inside jewels (s.), the sliding areas between levers, and the spring inside the barrel (requiring a special grease), as well as numerous other parts of a movement.

LUG (image 1)

Double extension of the case middle (s.) by which a strap or bracelet is attached. Normally, straps and bracelets are attached with removable spring bars.

LUMINESCENT (image 2)

Said of materials applied on markers (s.) and/or hands (s.), emitting the luminous energy previously absorbed as electromagnetic light rays. Tritium is no longer used and was replaced by other substances having the same emitting powers, but with virtually zero radioactivity, such as Super-LumiNova and Lumibrite.

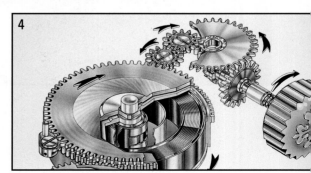

MAINSPRING (image 3)

This and the barrel (s.) make up the driving element of a movement (s.). It stores and transmits the power force needed for its functioning.

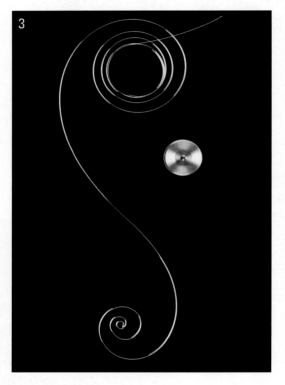

MANUAL (image 4)

A mechanical movement (v.) in which winding is performed by hand. The motion transmitted from the user's fingers to the crown is forwarded to the movement through the winding stem (s.), from this to the barrel (s.) through a series of gears (s.) and finally to the mainspring (s.).

MARINE CHRONOMETER

A large-sized watch enclosed in a box (therefore also called box chronometer) mounted on gimbals and used, on board of ships, to determine the respective longitude.

MARKERS

Elements printed or applied on the dial, sometimes they are luminescent (s.), used as reference points for the hands to indicate hours and fifteen- or five-minute intervals.

MEAN TIME
The mean time of the meridian of the Greenwich Observatory, considered the universal meridian, is used as a standard of the civil time system, counted from midnight to midnight.

MICROMETER SCREW (image 1)
Element positioned on the regulator, allowing to shift it by minimal and perfectly gauged ranges so as to obtain accurate regulations of the movement.

MICRO-ROTOR, s. Rotor. (image 2)

MINUTE REPEATER, s. Repeater.

MODULE (image 3)
Self-contained mechanism, independent of the basic caliber (s.), added to the movement (s.) to make an additional function available: chronograph (s.), power reserve (s.), GMT (s.), perpetual or full calendar (s).

MOONPHASE (image 3)
A function available in many watches, usually combined with calendar-related features. The moonphase disc advances one tooth every 24 hours. Normally, this wheel has 59 teeth and assures an almost perfect synchronization with the lunation period, i.e. 29.53 days (in fact, the disc shows the moonphases twice during a single revolution). However, the difference of 0.03 days, i.e. 44 minutes each month, implies the need for a manual adjustment every two and a half years to recover one day lost with respect to the real state of moonphase. In some rare case, the transmission ratio between the gears controlling the moonphase are calculated with extreme accuracy so as to require manual correction only once in 100 years.

MOVEMENT (image 1 - page 389)
The entire mechanism of a watch. Movements are divided into two great families: quartz and mechanical; the latter are available with manual (s.) or automatic (s.) winding devices.

MOVEMENT-BLANK s. Ebauche

NIVAROX
Trade name (from the producer's name) of a steel alloy, resisting magnetization, used for modern self-compensating balance springs (s.). The quality level of this material is indicated by the numeral following the name in decreasing value from 1 to 5.

OBSERVATORY CHRONOMETER
An observatory-tested precision watch that obtained the relevant rating certificate.

OPEN-FACE CALIBER s. Lépine Caliber.

OSCILLATION
Complete oscillation or rotation movement of the balance (s.), formed by two vibrations (s.).

OVERCOIL s. Balance spring.

PALLETS
Device of the escapement (s.) transmitting part of the motive force to the balance (s.), in order to maintain the amplitude of oscillations unchanged by freeing a tooth of the escape wheel at one time.

PAWL
Lever with a beak that engages in the teeth of a wheel under the action of a spring.

PILLAR-PLATE OR MAIN PLATE
Supporting element of bridges (s.) and other parts of a movement (s).

PINION
Combines with a wheel and an arbor (s.) to form a gear (s.). A pinion has less teeth than a wheel and transmits motive force to a

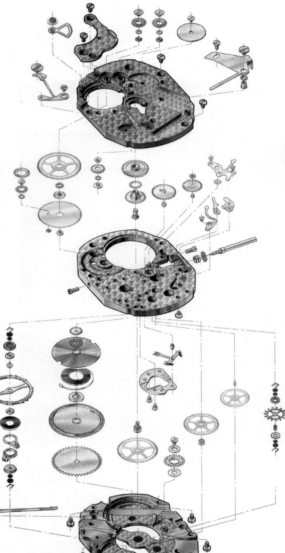

1

wheel. Pinion teeth (normally 6 to 14) are highly polished to reduce friction to a minimum.

PIVOT

End of an arbor (s.) turning on a jewel (s.) support. As their shape and size can influence friction, the pivots of the balance-staff are particularly thin and, hence, fragile, so they are protected by a shockproof (s.) system.

PLATE s. Pillar-plate.

PLATED

Said of a metal treated by a galvanizing procedure in order to apply a slight layer of gold or another precious metal (silver, chromium, rhodium or palladium) on a brass or steel base.

PLEXIGLAS

A synthetic resin used for watch crystal.

POINÇON DE GENÈVE (image 1)

Distinction assigned by the Canton of Geneva to movements produced by watchmaker firms of the Region and complying with all the standards of high horology with respect to craftsmanship, small-scale production, working quality, accurate assembly and setting. The Geneva Seal is engraved on at least one bridge and shows the Canton's symbol, i.e. a two-field shield with an eagle and a key respectively in each field.

POWER RESERVE (image 2)

Duration (in hours) of the residual functioning autonomy of a movement after it has reached the winding peak. The duration value is displayed by an instantaneous indicator: analog (hand on a sector) or digital (through a window). The related mechanism is made up of a series of gears linking the winding barrel and hand. Recently, specific modules were introduced which may be combined with the most popular movements.

PRECISION

Accuracy rate of a watch, a term difficult to define exactly.

Usually, a precision watch is a chronometer whose accuracy-standard is certified by an official watch-rating bureau, and a high-precision watch is a chronometer certified by an observatory.

PULSIMETER CHRONOGRAPH
The pulsimeter scale shows, at a glance, the number of pulse beats per minute. The observer releases the chronograph hand when starting to count the beats and stops at the 30th, the 20th or the 15th beat according to the basis of calibration indicated on the dial.

PUSHER, PUSH-PIECE or PUSH-BUTTON (image 1)
Mechanical element mounted on a case (s.) for the control of specific functions. Generally, pushers are used in chronographs (s.), but also with other functions.

PVD
Abbreviation of Physical Vapor Deposition, a plating process consisting of the physical transfer of substance by bombardment of electrons.

RATCHET (WHEEL)
Toothed wheel prevented from moving by a click pressed down by a spring.

RATING CERTIFICATES s. Chronometer and COSC.

REGULATING UNIT (image 2)
Made up by balance (s.) and balance spring (s.), governing the division of time within the mechanical movement, assuring its regular

1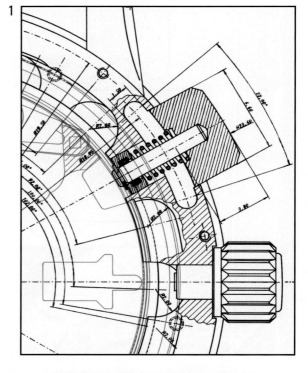

2

running and accuracy. As the balance works like a pendulum, the balance spring's function consists of its elastic return and starting of a new oscillation. This combined action determines the frequency, i.e. the number of vibrations per hour, and affects the rotation speed of the different wheels. In fact the balance, by its oscillations, at every vibration (through the action of the pallets), frees a tooth of the escape wheel (s. Escapement). From this, motion is transmitted to the fourth wheel, which makes a revolution in one minute, to the third and then the center wheel, the latter making a full rotation in one hour. However, everything is determined by the correct time interval of the oscillations of the balance.

REGULATOR (image 1)

Regulating the functioning of a movement by lengthening and shortening the active section of the balance spring (s.). It is positioned on the balance-bridge and encompasses the balance spring with its two pins near its fixing point on the bridge itself. By shifting the index, the pins also are moved and, by consequence, the portion of the balance spring capable of bringing the balance back is lengthened or shortened by its elastic force. The shorter it is, the more reactive it tends to be and the more rapidly it brings the balance back and makes the movement run faster. The contrary happens when the active portion of the balance spring is lengthened. Given today's high frequencies of functioning, even slight index shifts entail daily variations of minutes. Recently, even more refined index-regulation systems were adopted (from eccentric (s.) to micrometer screws (s.)) to limit error margins to very few seconds per day.

REMONTOIR, CONSTANT-FORCE

Old term used to denote any mechanism assuring a constant transmission of the driving power to the escape wheel.

REPEATER (image 2)

Mechanism indicating time by acoustic sounds. Contrary to the watches provided with en-passant sonnerie (s.) devices, that strike the number of hours automatically, repeaters work on demand by actuating a slide (s.) or pusher (s.)

positioned on the case side. Repeaters are normally provided with two hammers and two gongs: one gong for the minutes and one for the hours. The quarters are obtained by the almost simultaneous strike of both hammers. The mechanism of the striking work is among the most complex complications.

RETROGRADE (image 1)
Said of a hand (s.) that, instead of making a revolution of 360 before starting a new measurement, moves on an arc scale (generally of 90 to 180) and at the end of its trip comes back instantaneously. Normally, retrograde hands are used to indicate date, day or month in perpetual calendars, but there are also cases of retrograde hours, minutes or seconds. Unlike the case of the classical indication over 360, the retrograde system requires a special mechanism to be inserted into the basic movement.

ROLLER TABLE or ROLLER
Part of the escapement in the shape of a disc fitted to the balance staff and carrying the impulse pin that transmits the impulses given by the pallets to the balance.

ROTOR (image 2)
In automatic-winding mechanical movements the rotor is the part that, by its complete or partial revolutions and the movements of human arm, allows winding of the mainspring (s.).

SCALE (image 3)
Graduation on a measuring instrument, showing the divisions of a whole of values, especially on a dial, bezel. The scales mostly used in horology are related to the following measuring devices: tachometer (s.) (indicating the average speed), telemeter (s.) (indicating the distance of a simultaneously luminous and acoustic source, e.g. a cannon-shot or a thunder and related lightning), pulsometer (to calculate the total number of heartbeats per minute by counting only a certain quantity of them). For all of these scales, measuring starts at the beginning of the event concerned and stops at its end; the reading refers directly to the chronograph second hand, without requiring further calculations.

1

SECOND TIME-ZONE INDICATOR, s. GMT and World Time.

SECTOR, s. Rotor.

SELF-WINDING, s. Automatic.

SHOCKPROOF or SHOCK-RESISTANT (image 1)
Watches provided with shock-absorber systems (e.g. Incabloc) help prevent damage from shocks to the balance pivots. Thanks to a retaining spring system, it assures an elastic play of both jewels, thus absorbing the movements of the balance-staff pivots when the watch receives strong shocks. The return to the previous position is due to the return effect of the spring. If such a system is lacking, the shock forces exert an impact on the balance-staff pivots, often causing bending or even breakage.

SIDEREAL TIME
The conventional time standard refers to the sidereal year (defined in terms of an average of 365.25636 days) considered to be perfectly regular until very recently, but – even though this is not true – the difference is so slight that it is virtually neglected. As a unit of time, the sidereal day is used mainly by astronomers to define the interval between two upper transits of the vernal point in the plane of the meridian.

SKELETON, SKELETONIZED (image 2)
Watches whose bridges and pillar-plates are cut out in a decorative manner, thus revealing all the parts of the movement.

SLIDE (image 3)
Part of a mechanism moving with friction on a slide-bar or guide.

SMALL SECOND
Time display in which the second hand is placed in a small subdial.

3

SNAILING (image 4)
Decoration with a spiral pattern, mainly used on the barrel wheel or on big-sized full wheels.

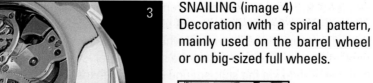

4

SOLAR TIME

Generally speaking, the time standard referred to the relative motion of the Earth and the Sun governing the length of day and night. The true solar day is the period measured after the Sun appears again in the same position from our point of observation. Due to the non-uniform rotation of the Earth around the Sun, this measure is not regular. As an invariable measure unit, the mean solar day corresponds to the average duration of all the days of the year.

SOLSTICE

The time when the sun is farthest from the equator, i.e. on June 21st (Summer solstice) and December 21st (Winter solstice).

SONNERIE (EN PASSANT)

Function consisting of an acoustic sound, obtained by a striking work made up of two hammers (s.) striking gongs (s.) at set hours, quarter- and half-hours. Some devices can emit a chime (with three or even four hammers and gongs). By a slide (s.) or an additional pusher (s.) it is possible to exclude the sonnerie device and to select a so-called grande sonnerie.

SPLIT-SECOND CHRONOGRAPH (image 1)

Chronographs with split-second mechanisms are particularly useful for timing simultaneous phenomena which begin at the same time, but end at different times, such as sporting events in which several competitors are taking part. In chronographs of this type, an additional hand is superimposed on the chronograph hand. Pressure on the pusher starts both hands, which remain superimposed as long as the split-second mechanism is not blocked. This is achieved when the split-second hand is stopped while the chronograph hand continues to move. After recording, the same pusher is pressed a second time, releasing the split-second hand, which instantly joins the still-moving chronograph hand, synchronizing with it, and is thus

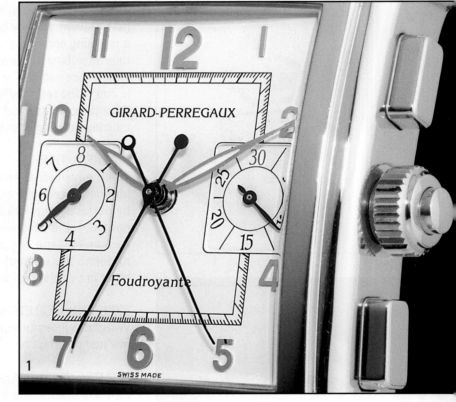

ready for another recording. Pressure on the return pusher brings the hands back to zero simultaneously, provided the split-second hand is not blocked. Pressure on the split pusher releases the split-second hand, which instantly joins the chronograph hand if the split-second hand happens to be blocked.

1

SPRUNG BALANCE (image 1)
Regulating organ consisting of the balance and the relevant spring.

STAFF or STEM, s. Arbor.

STOPWORK
Traditional device (now obsolete) provided with a finger piece fixed to the barrel arbor and a small wheel in the shape of a Maltese cross mounted on the barrel cover, limiting the extent to which the barrel (s.) can be wound.

STRIKING WORK, s. Sonnerie and Repeater.

SUBDIAL, s. Zone.

SUPER-LUMINOVA, s. Luminescent.

SWEEP SECOND HAND
A center second hand, i.e. a second hand mounted on the center of the main dial.

TACHOMETER or TACHYMETER (image 1)
Function measuring the speed at which the wearer runs over a given distance. The tachometer scale is calibrated to show the speed of a moving object, such as a vehicle, over a known distance. The standard length on which the calibration is based is always shown on the dial, e.g. 1,000, 200 or 100 meters, or—in some cases—one mile. As the moving vehicle, for instance, passes the starting-point of the measured course whose length corresponds to that used as the basis of calibration, the observer releases the chronograph hand and stops it as the vehicle passes the finishing point. The figure indicated by the hand on the tachometer scale represents the speed in kilometers or miles per hour.

TELEMETER (image 1)
By means of the telemeter scale, it is possible to measure the distance of a phenomenon that is both visible and audible. The chronograph hand is released at the instant the phenomenon is seen; it is stopped when the sound is heard, and its position on the scale shows, at a glance, the distance in kilometers or miles separating the phenomenon from the observer. Calibration is based upon the speed at which sound travels through the air, viz. approximately 340 meters or 1,115 feet per second. During a thunderstorm, the time that has elapsed between the flash of lightning and the sound of the thunder is registered on the chronograph scale.

THIRD WHEEL
Wheel positioned between the minutes and seconds wheels.

TIME ZONES
The 24 equal spherical lunes unto which the surface of the Earth

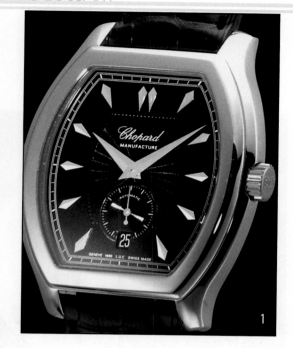

is conventionally divided, each limited by two meridians. The distance between two adjacent zones is 15° or 1 hour. Each country adopts the time of its zone, except for countries with more than one zone. The universal standard time is that of the zero zone whose axis is the Greenwich meridian.

TONNEAU (image 1)
Particular shape of a watchcase, imitating the profile of a barrel, i.e. with straight, shorter, horizontal sides and curved, longer, vertical sides.

TOURBILLON (image 2)
Device invented in 1801 by A. L. Breguet. This function equalizes position errors due to changing positions of a watch and related effects of gravity. Balance, balance spring and escapement are housed inside a carriage (s.), also called a cage, rotating by one revolution per minute, thus compensating for all the possible errors over 360. Although this device is not absolutely necessary for accuracy purposes today, it is still appreciated as a complication of high-quality watches.

TRAIN (image 3)
All the wheels between barrel (s.) and escapement (s.).

TRANSMISSION WHEEL s. Crown-wheel

UNIVERSAL TIME
The mean solar time (s.) of the Greenwich meridian, counted from noon to noon, Often confused with the mean time (s.) notion.

VARIATION
In horology the term is usually referred to the variation of the daily rate, i.e. the difference between two daily rates specified by a time interval.

WINDING, AUTOMATIC s. Automatic

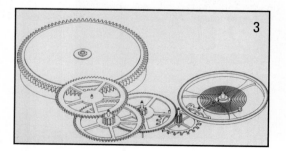

VIBRATION

Movement of a pendulum or other oscillating bodies, limited by two consecutive extreme positions. In an alternate (pendulum or balance) movement, a vibration is a half of an oscillation (s.). The number of hourly vibrations corresponds to the frequency of a watch movement, determined by the mass and diameter of a balance (s.) and the elastic force of the balance spring. The number of vibrations per hour (vph) determines the breaking up of time (the "steps" of a second hand). For instance, 18,000 vph equals a vibration duration of 1/5 second; in the same way 21,600 vph = 1/6 second; 28,800 vph = 1/8 second; 36,000 vph = 1/10 second. Until the 1950s, wristwatches worked mostly at a frequency of 18,000 vph; later, higher frequencies were adopted to produce a lower percentage of irregularities to the rate. Today, the most common frequency adopted is 28,800 vph, which assures a good precision standard and less lubrication problems than extremely high frequencies, such as 36,000 vph.

WATER RESISTANT or WATERPROOF (image 1)

A watch whose case (s.) is designed in such a way as to resist infiltration by water (3 atmospheres, corresponding to a conventional depth of 30 meters; 5 atmospheres, corresponding to a conventional depth of 50 meters.)

WHEEL

Circular element, mostly toothed, combines with an arbor (s.) and a pinion (s.) to make up a gear (s.). Wheels are normally made of brass, while arbors and pinions are made of steel. The wheels between barrel (s.) and escapement (s.) make up the so-called train (s.).

WINDING STEM

Element transmitting motion from the crown (s.) to the gears governing manual winding and setting.

WINDOW (image 2)

Aperture in the dial, that allows reading the underlying indication, mainly the date, but also indications concerning a second zone's time or jumping hour (s.).

1

WORLD TIME (image 1)
Additional feature of watches provided with a GMT (s.) function, displaying the 24 time zones on the dial or bezel, each zone referenced by a city name, providing instantaneous reading of the time of any country.

ZODIAC
Circular belt with the ecliptic in the middle containing the twelve constellations through which the sun seems to pass in the course of a year.

ZONE
Small additional dial or indicator that may be positioned, or placed off-center on the main dial, used for the display of various functions (e.g. second counters).

BRAND DIRECTORY

A. LANGE & SÖHNE
Altenberger Strasse 15
D-01768 Glashütte, Germany
Tel: 49 (0) 35053 440 - USA: 1 310 317 9852

ARNOLD & SON
Avenue Leopold-Robert 23
2300 La Chaux-de-Fonds, Switzerland
Tel: 41 32 910 90 62 - USA: 1 212 688 4550

AUDEMARS PIGUET
CH-1348 Le Brassus, Switzerland
Tel: 41 21 845 14 00 - USA: 1 212 688 6644

BAUME & MERCIER
Route de Chêne 61
1211 Geneva 29, Switzerland
Tel: 41 22 707 31 31 - USA: 1 212 909 6385

BLANCPAIN
Chemin de l'Etang 6
1094 Paudex, Switzerland
Tel: 41 21 796 36 36 - USA: 1 201 271 1400

BOVET FLEURIER SA
9 Rue Ami-Lévrier
CH 1207 Geneve, Switzerland
Tel: 41 21 731 46 38 - USA: 1 212 869 1888

BREGUET
1344 L'Abbaye, Switzerland
Tel: 41 21 841 90 90 - USA: 1 800 897 9477

BREITLING
Case Postale 1132
2540 Grenchen, Switzerland
Tel: 41 32 654 54 54 - USA: 1 203 762 1180

CARTIER INTERNATIONAL
51 Rue Pierre Charron
75008 Paris, France
Tel: 33 1 4218 4383 - USA: 1 800 227 8437

CHOPARD
Rue de Veyrot 8
1217 Meyrin-Geneva 2, Switzerland
Tel: 41 22 719 31 31 - USA: 1 800 821 0300

DE BETHUNE
6 Granges-Jaccard
1454 La Chaux L'Auberson, Switzerland
Tel: 41 24 454 22 81 - USA: 1 305 695 1435

de GRISOGONO
Route de St. Julien 176
1228 Plan-les-Ouates, Switzerland
Tel: 41 22 817 81 00 - USA: 1 212 821 0280

F. P. JOURNE
Rue de l'Arquebuse 17
1204 Geneva, Switzerland
Tel: 41 22 322 09 09 - USA: 1 305 531 2600

FRANCK MULLER
Rue de Malagny 22
1294 Genthod, Switzerland
Tel: 41 22 959 88 88 - USA: 1 212 463 8898

GERALD GENTA
34, Rue de Monruz
2008 Neuchatel, Switzerland
Tel: 41 32 722 78 78 - USA: 1 212 315 9700

GIRARD-PERREGAUX
Place Girardet 1
2301 La Chaux-de-Fonds, Switzerland
Tel: 41 32 911 33 33 - USA: 1 201 804 1978

GLASHÜTTE ORIGINAL
Altenberger Strasse 1
D-01768 Glashütte in Sachsen , Germany
Tel: 49 (0) 35034 6231

GRAHAM
Avenue Leopold-Robert 23
2300 La Chaux-de-Fonds, Switzerland
Tel: 41 32 910 90 62 - USA: 1 212 688 4550

GREUBEL FORSEY
19-21 Rue du Manège
2300 La Chaux-de-Fonds, Switzerland
Tel: 41 32 751 71 76
USA: 1 310 205 5555

GUY ELLIA
21 Rue de la Paix
Paris 75002 France
Tel: 33 1 53 30 25 25

HARRY WINSTON
Rue de Lausanne 82
1202 Geneva, Switzerland
Tel: 41 22 716 29 00 - USA: 1 212 245 2000

IWC
Baumgarten Strasse15
8201 Schaffhausen, Switzerland
Tel: 41 52 635 65 90 - USA: 1 212 891 2460

JAEGER-LeCOULTRE
Rue de la Golisse 8
1347 Le Sentier, Switzerland
Tel: 41 21 845 02 02 - USA: 1 212 308 2525

JAQUET DROZ
Rue Jaquet Droz 5
2300 La Chaux-de-Fonds, Switzerland
Tel: 41 32 911 28 88

PARMIGIANI FLEURIER
Rue du Temple 11
2114 Fleurier, Switzerland
Tel: 41 32 862 66 30
USA: 1 949 489 2885

PATEK PHILIPPE
Chemin du Pont du Centenaire 141
1228 Plan-les-Ouates, Switzerland
Tel: 41 22 884 20 20 - USA: 1 212 218 1240

PIAGET
Route du Chêne 61
1228 Plan-les-Ouates, Switzerland
Tel: 41 22 707 32 32 - USA: 1 212 355 6444

PIERRE KUNZ
22, Rue de Malagny
1228 Genthod, Switzerland
Tel: 41 22 959 88 88- USA: 1 212 463 8898

RGM
801 West Main Street
Mount Joy PA 17552 USA
Tel: 1 717 653 9799

RICHARD MILLE
11 Rue du Jura
2345 Les Breuleux Jura, Switzerland
Tel: 41 32 959 43 53 - USA: 1 310 205 5555

ROGER DUBUIS
Rue André-de-Garrini 2
CH-1217 Meyrin-Geneva, Switzerland
Tel: 41 22 783 28 28 - USA: 1 570 970 8888

ULYSSE NARDIN
3 Rue du Jardin
2400 Le Locle, Switzerland
Tel: 41 32 930 74 00 - USA: 1 561 988 8600

VACHERON CONSTANTIN
Rue des Moulins 1
1204 Geneva, Switzerland
Tel: 41 22 93 020 05
USA: 1 212 713 0707

ZENITH
2400 Le Locle, Switzerland
Tel: 41 32 930 62 62 - USA: 1 973 467 1890